PENGUIN CANADA

Green for Life

Award-winning broadcaster and writer GILLIAN DEACON brings her informed and friendly style to the subject that has long been her passion. A busy working mom and host of CBC-TV's *The Gill Deacon Show,* she understands the challenges of trying to "do it all" with a smaller environmental footprint.

GREEN FOR LIFE

200 Simple Eco-Ideas for Every Day

Gillian Deacon

PENGUIN
CANADA

PENGUIN CANADA

Published by the Penguin Group

Penguin Group (Canada), 90 Eglinton Avenue East, Suite 700,
Toronto, Ontario, Canada M4P 2Y3 (a division of
Pearson Canada Inc.)

Penguin Group (USA), 375 Hudson Street, New York,
New York 10014, U.S.A.
Penguin Books Ltd, 80 Strand, London WC2R 0RL, England
Penguin Ireland, 25 St. Stephen's Green, Dublin 2, Ireland
(a division of Penguin Books Ltd)
Penguin Group (Australia), 250 Camberwell Road, Camberwell,
Victoria 3124, Australia
(a division of Pearson Australia Group Pty Ltd)
Penguin Books India Pvt Ltd, 11 Community Centre, Panchsheel
Park, New Delhi – 110 017, India
Penguin Group (NZ), 67 Apollo Drive, Rosedale, North Shore 0632,
Auckland, New Zealand (a division of Pearson New Zealand Ltd)
Penguin Books (South Africa) (Pty) Ltd, 24 Sturdee Avenue,
Rosebank, Johannesburg 2196, South Africa

Penguin Books Ltd, Registered Offices: 80 Strand, London
WC2R 0RL, England

First published 2008

10 9 8 7 6 5 4 3 2 1 (OPM)

Copyright © Gillian Deacon, 2008

Manufactured in the U.S.A.

This book was printed on 100% PCW recycled paper

Library and Archives Canada Cataloguing in Publication data
available on request.

Visit Penguin Books' website at **www.penguin.ca**

Special and corporate bulk purchase rates available;
please see **www.penguin.ca/corporatesales**
or call 1-800-810-3104, ext 477 or 474.

It is better to light a single candle than to curse the darkness.

—Unknown

Contents

Introduction

> We should no longer accept the counsel of those who tell us that we must fill our world with poisonous chemicals; we should look about and see what other course is open to us.
>
> —Rachel Carson, *Silent Spring*, 1962

It has been nearly fifty years since the publication of *Silent Spring*, the book that launched the environmental movement as we know it today. And while we may point to any number of developments in science and technology, marvellous inventions and important laws that have significantly changed the world since 1962, it is only recently that we have begun to heed Rachel Carson's advice and look about to see what other course is open to us.

No one said the human species was quick to change.

Green is the new black

Now, even the most gluttonous consumer and the most stubborn skeptic can't deny the growing crisis emerging in every morning's headlines, every evening's news. Pollution, global warming, freak weather patterns, increasing cancer rates, endangered species lists—these are now the stories of our everyday lives.

The environment isn't what it used to be. No longer the domain of obscure wildlife biologists and anonymous scientific researchers, environmentalism is now playing out with a star-studded cast. Al Gore is not only the star of an Oscar-winning, top-grossing documentary about climate change, he is now also a Nobel laureate. Cameron Diaz and Leonardo DiCaprio lead a pack of A-list celebrities driving hybrid vehicles and beating the eco-drum. Mainstream manufacturers and retailers are scrambling to keep up with the rising demand for products that are made with environmental and social integrity—or to at least look like they are.

Organic evolution

So what does it mean to be an environmentalist now, if it's not just for science types and hippies anymore? I didn't study wildlife biology—heck, I only squeaked through grade nine biology; I was never chained before a bulldozer in protest at Clayoquot Sound or Temagami; I do not own a pair of Birkenstocks; I shave my underarms regularly; I have never hugged a tree. But I have become known as something of an environmentalist. So what does that mean?

To me, it simply means I have fused the war-baby values of my waste-not-want-not parents with the soul-stirring nature scenes I was fortunate enough to experience as a child at a cottage on the Ottawa River and a summer camp near Algonquin Park.

My mother taught me to recycle long before the trucks came to the curb, because it makes sense. My father taught me that you put on a sweater when you're cold instead of turning up the heat, because it makes sense. And when I came to realize that by doing simple things, economical things, usually, I could help preserve the clean air, fresh water and wildlife that, like so many Canadians, I felt defined by—well that did it. I was sold.

When I met my husband, it was his fiery rebellion, his questioning of authority—which was so attractive until I realized, too late, that my children would inherit this gene and make my life difficult—that galvanized my position even further. I began to question conventional wisdom. I began to discover a whole world out there of alternative products and independent thought. And as I scratched the surface a few short years ago, I began to discover other ways to live the life I love without hurting myself or the earth in the process.

It could happen to you

So that's my story. What about you? How did you become an environmentalist? I bet you didn't know you were an environmentalist, did you? But I'm telling you, you are. I can prove it. Answer true or false to the following questions:

1. I enjoy the sight of a sunset over still water.

2. I've noticed the brown haze over the city and feel a little creeped out about how it got there and what it means for the people breathing this air every day.

3. I feel relaxed when I spend time walking through the forest.

4. I hate the smell of the stuff I use to clean my bathtub and counters, and the fumes give me a headache.

5. The sight of children playing in an open field of wild-flowers is more appealing than seeing them play on concrete.

You see where I'm going with this, right? Not just for granola-heads anymore, tree hugging is a universal pleasure.

So you are an environmentalist, but you drive a car, need your microwave, can't live without imported brie and are a sucker for glossy magazines. You know what? It's okay. I drive a great car, a big, fast one too. And I drive kids to hockey practice and keep my house clean and try to keep up with fashions and trends. I renovated my kitchen, juggle freelance work to try to pay for it, and on a really good day, might even throw a dinner party.

I'm not that different from you, but I have a set of habits and tricks up my sleeve that make it easy to live a busy life in a much more sustainable way.

A connection to something bigger than you

I can almost guarantee you that paying more attention to the way you shop, eat and live is going to make you feel better. It will give you a sense of connection to the world you are part of—not in an "organics are all the rage" kind of way, but in an "I'm becoming part of the solution instead of just the problem" kind of way.

Neighbours and friends who have begun to green their life tell me they feel excited and energized by doing something they know is right. The active pursuit of something you believe in can be practically spiritual. You may not be able to see a greener planet, but you sure can believe in it.

After all, great spiritual masters throughout the ages have advocated compassion and looking outwards as the key to finding meaning in life. Being more environmentally aware does exactly that—it gives you a sense of higher purpose (looking out for Mother Earth), but it also provides purely selfish satisfaction (looking out for the health of you and your loved ones). And as often as not, living lighter on the earth will be lighter on your wallet too.

Another course is open to us

Most days, in spite of the soaring temperatures and the downward-spiralling air quality, I can at least rest a little easier knowing I am trying to make things better. It makes me feel like I am part of something. Isn't that something we all want to feel?

If you think that the little things you do in your own life couldn't possibly make a difference to the global environmental crisis, let me encourage you to think again. Every revolution begins with the slightest shift; when we all start to live with more consideration of the planet, living sustainably becomes the new normal. That shift is already happening—and I know you want to be part of it.

Call it what you like: environmentalism, sustainable living—or even green for life. By whatever name, it is a lifestyle for every one of us to embrace, as quickly and as intelligently as we are able, so that we may all continue to live the life we so cherish on this earth.

How to use this book

Most of us don't live off the grid or drive electric cars, but we do want to get involved and lighten our footprint on the earth. *Green for Life* is a great way to get started. It's a practical guide to living the life you love in a more sustainable way.

There are no gripping plot twists, no tear-jerking dramas. Except for the reference to hormone-free birth control, there are no steamy love scenes. *Green for Life* is for bite-sized consumption—it's not a book you are likely to read in a single sitting. The goal here is long-term behaviour change, and that's not likely to happen overnight. Take it one page at a time.

Flip through these chapters to find the activities in your life that you feel most ready to change. That article in the paper the other day about the environmental devastation caused by the tar sands got you thinking? Okay, turn to Chapter 12, "How to Drive a Car," to find greener ways to get where you want to go. Your children are developing allergy symptoms? Check out Chapter 1, "How to Make Dinner," and Chapter 21, "How to Raise Healthy Kids."

Along the way, you may uncover a few tidbits that intrigue you and lead to change in other aspects of your life. You might like the idea of saving money on your electricity and hot water bills, so you read "How to Wash the Dishes" and "How to Take a Shower." You might be daydreaming about a home renovation project, so before you get started you read "How to Renovate Your House" or "How to Decorate Your House."

Read it once, read it a lot. Keep it by your bedside, not up on a shelf. Put this book to darn good use—make *Green for Life* work for you!

I hope the information in this book has as positive an impact on your life as it has had on mine. I know I'm still greening my life more and more each day—just the other day I switched to toothbrushes with replaceable heads, and I've now got my kids hooked on fair trade hot chocolate (I'm still waiting for a locally manufactured, recyclable iPod).

Good luck on your journey.

[1]
How to **Make Dinner**

Whether we break bread with the family, the cat or the evening news, we all have to eat. And these days, we can eat pretty much whatever our little hearts desire. Arabian kumquats? Aisle two. Smoked emu? Aisle four, right next to the marinated sea turtle. The only thing more complex than the array of choices we're faced with in the grocery aisles is the impact of our decisions around food. Will the kids eat it? Is it full of additives that will make them hyper? Will it make us fat or give us cancer? How far did it travel to get to our plates? Which creatures died so we could eat it?

Getting dinner to the table every night has never been more fraught with peril and complications. But before you throw up your oven mitts in exasperation, here are a few simple truths that will guide you to happier, healthier meal preparation.

#1 Eat less meat

Your mother told you to eat your vegetables. You probably tell your kids the same thing. What you can tell yourself is this: it takes seven times the amount of agricultural land and resources to produce a meat-based meal than it does to produce the equivalent nutritional value in a plant-based meal.

In Canada, we eat more than our share of meat—twice the global average. After car use, the amount of meat we eat has the next biggest impact on the environment. Are you ready for this?

THE SCARE:

Fully 16 percent of the world's greenhouse gases come from the methane tooted out by flatulent livestock—and methane is 23 times worse for the atmosphere than carbon dioxide.

→ Grazing lands take up more than a quarter of all the ice-free land on the planet.

→ One-third of the earth's land surface that was once wildlife habitat is now occupied by livestock.

→ Barns and slaughterhouses demand enormous amounts of energy to operate.

→ Fertilizers and manure contaminate the water system.

→ Antibiotics and growth hormones in animal feed are contributing to human disease.

But, you may be asking, how can I give up Sunday roasts, Christmas turkeys and BLTs?

You don't have to give up meat whole hog (as it were), just go meatless as often as you can. David Suzuki challenges Canadians to eat meat-free meals one day per week (take the Nature Challenge at www.davidsuzuki.org).

If you want to join the vegetarian train, hop on board! Not only will you cut down on your grocery bills, but you'll avoid some of the health concerns related to a meat-rich diet. We now know that meat is a major contributor to obesity, cancer and heart disease. Worried about feeling weak and sickly? I have been a vegetarian since 1987 and I feel great. And don't just take it from me. It was no lesser a mind than Albert Einstein who said, "Nothing will benefit human health and increase chances for survival of life on earth as much as the evolution to a vegetarian diet."

For more recipes, restaurant suggestions and other ideas on eating your veggies, check out www.veg.ca and www.veganoutreach.org.

#2 Eat local

It's the new organic. If there's one thing that organic awareness (see #3, below) has taught us, it's to pay attention to the story behind the food we eat. And what we now see is the long, energy-intensive journey our food often takes to get to our plates. Time was, 85 percent of the food we ate in this country was grown here, and 15 percent was imported. Today, those numbers are reversed.

So what? You like having strawberries and grapes all year long? Hear me out. Locally sourced food means fewer greenhouse gas emissions to transport it from the field to your table, requires less packaging to protect it during transporting, and is much better for you. Fruits and vegetables lose their nutrients with every passing day after

> **GRASS, NOT GRAIN** For those times when you do crave meat, try to source it from a local farm, where it was organically raised. And if you really want to make a smart meat choice, choose grass-fed beef. Most cows are grain fed, which plumps them up faster but doesn't suit their natural digestion whatsoever. Farmers have to use antibiotics to manage the cows' reaction to grain feed, which can lead to health risks for those of us higher up the food chain who are consuming the meat. For more on this, and a hugely compelling read, pick up Michael Pollan's wonderful book *The Omnivore's Dilemma*, or check out www.backtonaturebeef.com.

they're picked; eating local means you eat it sooner, and the difference in taste is incredible. Just compare a California strawberry to a locally grown strawberry in June.

And if you've been jumping on board the organics movement as your best bet for eco-friendly eating, consider this. "Certified organic" (see #3, below) means a product was grown without genetic engineering and without chemical herbicides or pesticides. It means animals were never fed growth hormones or antibiotics. It does not, however, tell you anything about the sustainability of the production standards on the farm your food came from. Eating locally, ideally shopping at your local farmers' market, is the single best way to ensure a healthy future for Canadian farmers and to support a local food economy.

If the environmental argument seems too abstract, consider this alarming scenario, one that is typical of most large communities in Canada: Toronto, even though it is surrounded by the bountiful farmlands of Southern Ontario, currently imports most of its food supply. This means that in the event of a major emergency blocking access to the city—such as a weather or transport crisis, or an act of terrorism—Toronto would have only enough food to feed its citizens for *three days*.

Recently, two Vancouverites put our long-distance dependence to the test. For one year, James MacKinnon and Alisa Smith ate only food produced within a hundred-mile radius of their home in Vancouver. They sure missed coffee and chocolate, but they swear they never felt better. Read *The 100-Mile Diet*, or try it yourself. Check out www.100milediet.org.

FOOD SHOPPING RULE OF THUMB When grocery shopping, remember: first choice is local organic, second choice is local non-organic, third choice is imported organic, fourth choice is imported non-organic.

Of course, it can be tricky to know how to eat locally and with the seasons, especially in our cold Canadian climate. For help figuring out what is local and in season where you live, check out www.eattheseasons.com. It'll give you some ideas about what to plan for dinner this week, and what to look for in the produce aisle.

 ## Eat organic

I knew the movement was really taking off when an organic produce section popped up in the tiny grocery store near my family's cottage in Northern Ontario. What I didn't know was *how much* it was taking off. In fact, 22 million Canadians bought organic foods at least once in the year 2000, which means you've probably heard the organic buzz already. But organic farming has been officially around in Canada since 1953, when a filmmaker (of all things) founded the Canadian Organic Soil Association. It was his response to the surge of chemicals developed for military purposes that were then expanded into agricultural and domestic use. For a few decades, the movement enjoyed quiet, slow growth, and then, boom! In the last five years, organics have grown by 130 percent. According to a Datamonitor report, the global organic food market generated more than $36 billion in 2006.

I know what you're thinking: I'll bet it did, with prices like that! But let's consider short-term versus long-term costs. Farmers who start with genetically modified seeds and use industrial methods to spray chemical pesticides and fertilizers usually get a larger yield and so can charge lower prices for their crops. Conversely, farms that use more old-fashioned (and chemical-free) methods, which involve crop rotation, companion planting and natural fertilizers, have the opposite result: higher labour costs, slower returns and lower yields.

But industrial farming practices strip the soil of precious nutrients for growing. To continue harvesting on large-scale farms, these operations have to apply greater and greater amounts of fertilizers (which travel far and wide at the whim of the wind and seldom reach their target). And as bugs become resistant to the pesticides, farmers have to spray more chemicals, many of which are toxic to humans.

The long-term health costs to those farm workers don't show up on the price of your apple, but they do show up in your taxes for health care. Healthier human workers earning a fair wage to weed their crops by hand—*that* shows up on the price of your organic apple. And you don't have to be spraying pesticides for a living to be adversely affected by them. A 2003 medical study in the UK showed that women with breast cancer are five to nine times more likely to have pesticide residues in their blood than those who are cancer free. We may eat only trace amounts of herbicides and insecticides on the peels of our fruits and veggies, but the combination is downright toxic—a little toxaphene on your tomatoes, a dash of parathion on your potatoes, mixed with a pinch of cypermethrin from your apples for good measure, and you've got a chemical cocktail that you wouldn't wish on your worst enemy. But it's probably in the food you eat every day if you're not serving organic.

Still looking for a reason to pay a little more for organics? Organic foods have significantly higher levels of vitamin C, magnesium, iron, antioxidants, essential fatty acids and all kinds of other good things.

Unfortunately, most of us don't have a grocery budget that will accommodate the extra cost of organic foods. So we often have to be judicious about where we spend extra money when buying organic.

Here are a few things to consider while shopping in the grocery aisles:

Kids

The children in your life—who actually eat more fresh fruit than us big kids—should definitely be eating organic whenever possible. Children are at an even greater risk from pesticides because they eat more food relative to their body weight and their nervous systems are still developing.

In 1993 the U.S. National Academy of Sciences conducted laboratory tests on eight popular baby foods. They found carcinogens, neurotoxins, endocrine disruptors and other highly dangerous chemicals in more than half of the samples. You'll find lots of organic baby food options on the store shelves these days. Or, you can take the cheaper route that I took with my little ones. Spend a rainy afternoon steaming up organic fruits and veggies in large quantities. Purée them, then pour the cooled mixture into ice-cube trays and place them in the freezer. Instant mini-portions, no neurotoxins.

Dairy

Milk and other dairy products are a great place to start with organics. There's no denying that organic dairy products carry the steepest price difference. But keep in mind that many toxic chemicals—including endocrine disruptors, which wreak havoc with human hormones—are stored in fat. All that glorious rich, creamy dairy goodness we love is, after all, animal-based fat. Considering how much milk kids drink, and how much butter and cheese and yogurt adults consume, it makes good sense from a health standpoint to pay a few extra dollars a week if you can, and make it organic.

Bananas

Where would your breakfast smoothie be without the glorious banana? Bananas are considered safer from pesticides since we always remove that thick protective peel before eating them. And at about 33 cents a pound, they're a potassium-packed bargain, right? But peel back the story and there's more to it. If we're paying that little at the end of the line, imagine how cheaply bananas are being produced at the other end. Banana workers are basically slave labourers. So even though the pesticides don't affect us as consumers, indentured workers are being paid a pittance and damaging their health with all those pesticides. In Costa Rica, where many of our bananas come from, only 5 percent of cultivated land is used for banana plantations, but they account for fully 35 percent of that country's pesticide imports. Make mine an organic fair trade banana smoothie, thanks.

To become more educated about organics, find good sources of organic food and learn how to support the organic farmers in your area, check out the Canadian Organic Growers' site at www.cog.ca.

---

20 FOODS TO BUY ORGANIC While reports vary on how to prioritize your organic shopping, the Environmental Working Group has compiled a reliable list of the 20 most highly pesticide-sprayed food crops:

Peaches	Spinach
Apples	Potatoes
Sweet bell peppers	Carrots
Celery	Green beans
Nectarines	Hot peppers
Strawberries	Cucumbers
Cherries	Raspberries
Lettuce	Plums
Grapes—imported	Oranges
Pears	Grapes—domestic (U.S.)

You can download a handy wallet-sized copy of this list at EWG's food news site, www.foodnews.org.

ORGANICS AT YOUR DOORSTEP **In larger municipalities, organics delivery services are taking off, bringing organic goodness straight to your door. In addition to providing convenience, these delivery services buy their organics in large quantities and ship directly to you, so their prices are much more reasonable than you might think. Check out:**

www.eatit.ca (Winnipeg),
www.frontdoororganics.com (Toronto),
www.hgof.ns.ca (Halifax),
www.equiterre.org (Montreal),
www.organicsathome.com (Vancouver),
www.freshorganics.ca (Calgary and Edmonton),
www.spud.ca (British Columbia and Calgary), and
www.new-terra-natural-food.com (Ottawa),
or search the Web for an organic food delivery service in your area.

#4 Beware the catch of the day

Fish is a nutritious source of protein and omega-3 fatty acids. That much we know. After that, trying to figure out which fish caught from which coast is safe for what age and how often you should eat it gets murkier than the river bottom at sundown. One thing is for sure: roughly 75 percent of the world's fisheries are either overfished or just fished out. So be mindful of how often you eat fish, and be sure you are choosing something that is sustainably harvested.

Now, unless you're just finishing up your doctoral thesis in marine biology (and even then), you probably aren't up to speed on the intimate details of the state of the world's oceans. If only there were a handy little list you could keep in your pocket or your wallet ...

In fact, there are several, and you can get them all free through the Endangered Fish Alliance (EFA). The EFA is a Canadian organization that helps chefs and fish markets stay abreast of the latest information and make responsible choices. They also have a consumer section on their website (go to www.endangeredfishalliance.org, then click on "Take Action") where you can download any one of the cards, including Environmental Defence Canada's excellent Pocket Seafood Selector, or the popular Seafood Watch card from a giant in marine research, the Monterey Bay Aquarium. The Seafood Watch program is updated regularly, categorizing best choices, good alternatives and what to avoid altogether.

Depending on what fish you're eating, it's important to know whether they are farmed or wild caught. Fish farms, or aquaculture, were designed to help solve the problem of depleted fish stocks. But, as we all know, sometimes those science experiments go a little haywire. Many fish farms rely on wild fish either for egg supply or as feed for their farmed stock, so they deplete the ocean's natural supply anyway. Fish farms are usually located along the natural shoreline, with net pens filled with thousands of fish kept like cattle in feedlots. So many fish in a concentrated area makes for an awful lot of fish waste, which pollutes the water, harming both the farmed and wild fish in the area. Antibiotics used to control those diseases also leak out into the surrounding environment and mess up the ecosystem permanently.

Salmon farms are some of the worst offenders, so try to avoid farmed salmon. According to the Institute for Health and Environment at the University at Albany, farmed fish has about 10 times the concentration of PCBs, dioxins and pesticides that wild salmon has.

Mussels, clams and oysters are okay to eat farmed; they require pristine waters to grow, so these fish farms usually do a lot to protect coastal waters in their area. Catfish, tilapia and trout are also safe choices as they are usually farmed inland, away from where wild fish feed and breed.

Regardless of where they were caught and by whom, fish come with a disturbing contamination of methylmercury, mostly from the emissions spewed by coal-fired electricity plants. The higher up the fish is on the marine food chain, the higher the level of mercury it contains. It's an ironic twist, the combination of benefits and dangers posed by eating fresh fish. Health Canada's recommendations are too complex to list here; check their website to see for yourself, especially if you are pregnant, nursing, or feeding children under the age of 15 (www.hc-sc.gc.ca/index_e.html).

My personal solution to the confusion? I feed my kids wild-caught canned tuna or salmon, no more than once a month, and I pay a little extra for RainCoast Trading brand from British Columbia. They catch with hooks, not nets, so no dolphins are caught in the haul, and they test all their fish for mercury levels. Well worth the extra dollar a month for tunafish sandwiches. I don't eat fish myself, having been a vegetarian for more than 20 years (see #1, above, for more on meatless meals).

Remember that you can be green for life at a restaurant too. Ask the waiters if the fish on the menu is wild caught or farmed. Ask if they know how the wild fish was caught. If they can't answer your questions, best to order something else. Just by asking, you've brought some awareness to the issue. You could even ask to speak to the manager or chef, to let them know that you care about the health of the world's oceans, and you think they should too. Pull out your handy-dandy Pocket Seafood Selector wallet card, listing endangered fish to avoid and sustainably harvested ones to choose—offer it to the maître d' as a peace gesture. Then enjoy the rest of your night out, feeling proud that you've begun to change the world.

 ## Eat fresh

Stop and think about how many fresh, raw crunchy things you've eaten today. For optimal nutrition, one-third of your diet should be raw. Some people eat nothing but raw food, citing how much nutrition is lost during the heating process.

Do the math on your own diet, and see how much of your food comes from the quick 'n' easy department—a box or a can or the freezer.

I have a pet name for the foods of modern convenience, though it's hardly affectionate: the Sinister Ps. They are, in very particular order, *processed*, (over)*packaged* and *prepared*. (For more on avoiding the other Sinister P, *portioned*, see Chapter 22, "How to Pack School Lunches.")

Processed food is really a misnomer—it's hardly food, really. Oh sure, that frozen dinner started out with recognizable ingredients, but there are so many artificial colourants and flavours added in there, it's hard to know what to call it anymore. Many of those preservatives and dyes that make popsicles purple, cookies less crumbly, or even kids' medicines fruit flavoured are derived from petroleum. And as appetizing as that might sound, it's just not good for you. Nutritionists say the sodium alone in processed foods is contributing to the threefold increase in cases of childhood diabetes over the last 30 years. Even type 2 diabetes, usually an adult-onset disease, is now starting to affect children.

The microwave actually furthers the problem in some processed foods. Research has also shown that in frozen prepared foods like pizza, french fries, waffles, popcorn and breaded fish, potentially toxic molecules are released into the foods from the packaging, which is designed to help brown food during microwaving.

Packaging is a big problem too. If we didn't have enough reasons already to dislike prepared processed foods, the stuff it comes wrapped in is the icing on the cake. Canadians throw away about half a kilogram of packaging every day. And if you're buying foods wrapped in plastic, then sheathed in freezer foil and cased in a cardboard box, you're probably beating that average.

If the staggering amount of garbage sent to landfills every day isn't depressing enough to turn you off packaged food, how about what it's doing to your health? The plastic coating inside your canned foods probably contains bisphenol A, a plasticizing chemical that has been closely linked with decreased sperm production, altered immune function, hyperactivity, recurrent miscarriages, and breast and prostate cancer. The U.S. Environmental Working Group recently tested canned foods for bisphenol A and found the highest levels in chicken soup, ravioli and infant formula. In some cases, they found that a single serving contained bisphenol A at two hundred times the government's safe levels for industrial chemicals.

The plastic wrap on your, well, *everything* probably contains the plasticizer DEHA, which is linked to negative effects on the liver, kidney, spleen and bone formation, and is classified as a possible human carcinogen. And the grease-proof paper and packaging used to contain oily foods like microwave popcorn, frozen pizzas and a lot of fast foods probably contains PFOA, classified by the U.S. Environmental Protection Agency (EPA) as a "likely human carcinogen."

Certainly makes you rethink the "convenience" of that microwavable meal; makes you want to haul out a raw carrot and call it dinner, doesn't it? I know, for some people, that's about the extent of their cooking skills. You don't have to become a gourmet chef overnight. Just include as much fresh produce in your meals as possible. And for help figuring out what is fresh and in season, check out www.eattheseasons.com.

#6 Avoid genetic engineering

Easy to say, but it's hard to do these days. Canada is one of the three major genetically modified organism (GMO) producers in the world, a dubious honour by my lights. In a confusing twist, the Health Canada website actually describes GMO foods this way: "foods resulting from a process not previously used for food; products that do not have a history of safe use as food." Which is a little weird, since Health Canada is also approving GMO foods for public consumption.

Genetically modified organisms are simply life forms that have been genetically engineered (GE), which means that scientists have crossbred a plant, taking DNA from one species and breeding it into another. Certain crops have been modified to be more resistant to pests—especially corn, soy and canola, in this country—or to be more nutritionally enriched—such as provitamin A–enhanced rice.

You can see how that sounds like a good thing. But there's more to the story. The plot thickens with more shady characters and mad scientists than in an old science fiction B movie. Like the one who is injecting jellyfish DNA into a species of conifer to make a Christmas tree that glows (that's fact, not film, by the way). Or the GMO corn injected with bacteria that kills monarch butterfly larvae as well as corn crop pests.

The idea of being able to trick Mother Nature by doctoring up these plants to resist pests—you know she's smarter than that! All that happens when you make a stronger plant is you get stronger pests. It's called evolution—word on the street is it's been going on for a while.

GMO foods are certainly not delivering on their golden promise. So far, GMO crops are requiring the same or higher amounts of pesticides, and they're producing no higher yields. What they *are* producing is a whole new strain of allergens. Most of us know someone who's suddenly developed hay fever or food allergies they've never had before. Makes you wonder why.

Even if you're buying all your tofu strictly organic, you're not out of the woods. Roughly 75 percent of processed foods contain GMO ingredients. Wouldn't you like to see that on the label of your frozen foods or packaged crackers? Well, you're not alone. In 2001, 93 percent of Canadians said they wanted mandatory labelling of GMO products. Give the people what they want? Not exactly. All these years later, we still have product labelling on a voluntary basis—*if* the manufacturer feels like it and *if* the product contains more than 5 percent GMO material. Most other countries have a limit of 1 percent! Contact the Department of Agriculture and Agri-Food to tell them it makes you mad (info@agr.gc.ca). Tell them you don't want to be part of a national science experiment. Ask them why foods that "do not have a history of safe use as food" are being sold to Canadians every day.

GET THE GE GUIDE Since GMO products aren't labelled as such, informing yourself about genetically engineered foods can be difficult, but it's getting easier. For example, Greenpeace has created a shopping guide entitled "How to Avoid Genetically Engineered Food." It's a catalogue of the GE foods sold on Canadian store shelves, with suggestions for alternatives. Download it from http://gmoguide.greenpeace.ca.

#7 Don't microwave plastic

With 75 percent greater energy efficiency over conventional ovens, your microwave is likely the best energy-saving device in your kitchen. So on the one hand, it is green for life indeed.

But be careful to use it wisely. Never heat any plastic wraps or containers in your microwave. Most plastics are made using petroleum-based chemicals that can leach out of the plastic and into your food. Research has shown that leaching increases when the plastic comes into contact with oily or fatty foods during heating, and from old or scratched plastic. (By the way, "microwave safe" does *not* mean that there is no leaching of chemicals.)

Avoid clingy plastic wraps too, especially if they're touching the food. A better alternative is waxed paper (check out www.chefsselect.com for biodegradable parchment and soy-waxed paper) or paper towel to cover your foods in the microwave. Some researchers go so far as to recommend slicing off a thin layer of deli food that is plastic wrapped, to avoid eating the part that's been in direct contact with the plastic. (Another reason to bring your own bags to the grocery store to avoid plastic contact with your food. See Chapter 14, "How to Go Shopping," for more on reusable shopping bags.)

So whether it's from your dishwasher, your microwave or even the leftovers you're transferring from the hot pan to the fridge, heat is a bad combination with any plastic container. Ikea, Canadian Tire and many other retailers now sell glass food storage containers in various sizes.

The other concern with microwaving, of course, is how much nutritional value in the food is lost during cooking. Steaming your broccoli tonight will leave 11 percent of its powerful antioxidants behind in the saucepan; microwaving it will destroy fully 97 percent of its antioxidants.

I've never owned a microwave, so I guess I'll never know what I might have done with all the extra time it's supposed to save. But I have managed just fine without one: I reheat in a cast-iron pan or using a metal steamer.

#8 Make your chocolate fair trade

Dinner just doesn't seem complete without a little hit of indulgence to wrap it up, does it? Preferably one involving chocolate. Chocolate brownies fresh from the oven can make you drool just thinking about them, and a squirt of chocolate syrup takes a bowl of ice cream right over the top.

If you are one of the millions of chocolate addicts out there, brace yourself, this news is going to be hard to take. Chocolate is harvested in such awful conditions by child labourers using deadly chemicals, it makes your blood run cold.

Veteran journalist Carol Off came on *The Gill Deacon Show* to talk about her book *Bitter Chocolate*, and I haven't looked at a chocolate chip cookie the same way since. Her research took her to Ivory Coast in West Africa, where about 70 percent of the world's chocolate comes from. Child slavery on cocoa farms there has been well documented, not just by Carol, but by no less than the U.S. State Department. And for all their work spraying industrial chemicals, many of which are banned for agricultural use in Canada, and labouring in dangerous conditions, the average West African working on a cocoa farm will take home less than $100 a year. Some of us spend more than that on chocolate in a single month.

For an eye-opening look at the dark story behind one of our favourite sweets, read *Bitter Chocolate*. In the meantime, be sure to buy fair trade chocolate products whenever you can. The Canadian company Cocoa

Camino imports fairly traded organic chocolate—check out www.lasiembra.com for more information.

#9 Don't use non-stick cookware

If you're looking for an excuse to go shopping, this is it. Your non-stick frying pans all need to be replaced. Simply put, the chemicals used to make them non-stick are so incredibly bad for you that no amount of scrubbing and sweating to get fried egg off cast iron could make it worth it to use non-stick. Cookware is "non-stick" by virtue of a chemical bath, a coating of perfluorochemicals to be precise, whose molecular structure causes them to repel both water and oil. The Environmental Working Group in Washington, D.C., says these chemicals are even worse than DDT—the now-banned pesticide that you might say begat the entire environmental movement in the 1960s. These chemicals never break down, which means they are in every single one of us; Health Canada tests in 2004 found them in every one of their test subjects.

So serious a concern are these chemicals that corporate giant 3M, makers of Post-it Notes, announced in 2000 they would be phasing out perfluorooctane sulfonate (PFOS), which was used in Scotchgard, the stain repellent most people have on their rugs and furniture, and perfluorooctanoic acid (PFOA), used to make non-stick coatings.

You *know* this is a serious problem when even the big profit makers say those chemicals are just too hazardous for the environment and for human health! Even polar bears in the Arctic have skyrocketing levels of PFOS in what little fat tissue they have left (if the warming temperatures don't kill them through lean winter feeding seasons, the chemicals we send them through our air and water streams just might). Imagine what is accumulating in human tissue after all those years of fried eggs cooked on Teflon.

So, get rid of your non-stick pots and pans pronto. Your best alternatives are stainless steel and cast iron. I've made the switch and never looked back.

(Hint: Cook's trick for cast iron—don't use soap when you wash it, just scrub it well and put it away dry. Your pans will be better "seasoned" by avoiding soap, so they'll be less-stick if not non-stick.)

#10 Make sure your kitchen appliances are green for life

Oven

Although they cost a little more at the outset, self-cleaning ovens will definitely save you money (and energy) in the end. Self-cleaning ovens are usually better insulated than standard ovens, which means that every time you cook you use less heat and less energy, saving money and the earth at the same time.

You've paid to get all that heat into your oven, so don't let it out by peeking! Look in the oven window to check your food—opening the door to peek lets 20 percent of the heat escape.

To make sure the oven door is doing its job keeping all that heat in, here are a couple of quick DIY tests. Close the oven door on a piece of paper—it should hold in place fairly snugly. If it is loose and easy to slide out, or it slips out on its own, your seals need to be replaced. Or, turn on your windup LED flashlight (see Chapter 28, "How to Plan a Holiday," for more on green for life flashlights) and put it in the oven and close the door. If you can see light shining through around the edges, you need to replace the door seals. (Remember to take the flash-light out so you won't have a smelly surprise the next time you preheat your oven!)

Stove

For stovetop cooking, be sure to match your pot to the size of the element—that is, the base of the pot should just cover the electric coil or gas ring. Pots that are smooth and flat on the bottom will cook food more quickly and efficiently because they make full contact with the heating element. Plus, your food will cook more evenly.

Once your water has come to a boil, turn down the heat. Turning the heat up to high won't cook your food any faster.

> **PUT ON THE PRESSURE** Pressure cookers are back, and with an environmental seal of approval. By cooking food in roughly one-third the time of conventional cooking methods, pressure cookers mean way less energy is used for meal prep—70 percent less, according to certain man-ufacturers. Invest in a good one because it will pay for itself in energy savings!

Fridge

Don't waste energy when you are hungry. Decide what you want from the fridge, *then* open the door to get it out.

You can also put a thermometer in your fridge to make sure you aren't spending extra money and using extra energy to keep it colder than necessary. Adjust the temperature until it runs between 3 and 5 degrees Celsius. This is as cold as it needs to be to prevent bacterial growth for food safety while still being energy efficient.

And just as you want that heat to stay inside your oven, you want the cold to stay in your fridge. Try the same paper or flashlight tests on the rubber door seals (see Oven section, above) to make sure you're not throwing your refrigeration money out the window. Keeping the seals wiped clean will also help them work better.

A few times a year, pull the fridge out from the wall and clean the condenser coils at the back. Dust and pet hair and all those other back-of-appliance mystery substances build up on the coils, which makes the motor work harder, which uses more electricity, which makes you have to work harder to pay for it all.

If your fridge is positioned in direct sunlight or next to a hot oven or dishwasher, it is going to have to work harder to stay cold. The more airflow around the fridge, the better. It allows the heat from the motors and compressors to escape. If the heat is trapped, the fridge has to work twice as hard to achieve a cool temperature inside.

Freezer

Let's face it, if you're going to make your food green for life by buying in bulk and buying in season and making homemade food, you're going to need a place to put it all.

So as much as I would like to be a one-fridge family, it just isn't happening—at least not until my three ravenous boys have flown the coop. In the meantime, there is a right way and a wrong way to have a second basement fridge or freezer.

Don't just put your old fridge downstairs for beer and extra freezer space. A fridge or freezer from the 1980s uses three times as much energy as a new one, and one from the 1990s nearly twice as much.

At our house, we have just made the switch to a new chest freezer. Chest freezers (with the lid on the top) are more efficient because lifting the door upwards to open releases less cold air. Labelling your foods clearly with a bold black marker when you put them in will mean easy retrieval later—so the door will be open for the least amount of time. Remember to leave about five centimetres between the freezer and the wall to allow air to circulate around it.

Take your freezer's temperature just like you did with your fridge (see above)—it should be set to –18 degrees Celsius for maximum efficiency. When you're putting any foods away in the freezer (or fridge), make sure they have cooled off. Warm foods in there will raise the temperature and make the cooling motor work harder, using more electricity.

If you are shopping for new appliances, make sure they are Energy Star models. Check out the federal government's information page on Energy Star ratings for more details, at www.oee.nrcan.gc.ca/energystar/.

[2]
How to **Wash the Dishes**

No matter how the dishwashing duties break down at your house, you don't have to get dishpan hands anymore. If you've been debating whether to invest in an automatic dishwasher, let the earth be your reason to make the change. Automatic dishwashers use way less water than washing by hand in the sink. Researchers in Germany pitted the most frugal and judicious handwashing against the modern automatic dishwasher and found that dishpan hands are the least of the problem. The dishwasher uses half the energy and one-sixth of the water compared with handwashing. Less soap too.

So, now that you're sold on the automatic washer, here's the greenest way to operate it.

#1 Be an Energy Star

Be sure to buy an Energy Star model to get the most for your money. An Energy Star washer can save you up to $100 in water over its lifetime and an additional $30 every year on your electrical bills. Dishwasher technology is evolving so quickly, you'd think by now they'd have invented a unit that loads itself. Today's dishwashers use

> **FILL IT UP** Be sure the dishwasher is full before you turn it on. Using all that energy to heat and dry just a few dishes is such a waste.

95 percent less energy than those built in the early 1970s. But *Consumer Reports* found that those fancy "smart" washers with dirt sensors used significantly more energy than the non-sensor types, and so it recommends skipping that jazzy feature when you're machine shopping.

#2 Run your dishwasher during off-peak hours

Once your dishwasher is fully loaded, don't feel you have to run it right away. Look for a model that comes with a delay setting. In the near future, it will pay to run major appliances during off-peak hours, as more and more utility companies convert to time-of-use billing. For example, by 2010, every home in Ontario will be equipped with a smart electricity meter, which will charge users higher electricity rates during peak hours. If you run your dishwasher at midnight, it will cost you—and the earth—a lot less, as the grid won't need to draw from coal-fired plants at that hour to keep up with demand. So to save on greenhouse gas emissions *and* on your electricity bill, run your dishwasher in the middle of the night and wake up to a clean load.

DON'T BE A WATER WASTER Much of the world gets by on 2.5 litres of water a day—running the water at the kitchen sink for two minutes uses more than *7 litres* of water. When I'm washing those pots and pans and other items that don't go in the dishwasher, I try to imagine that someone from an impoverished developing nation is standing there watching me. It sounds goofy, but it actually helps draw my attention to how much I leave the tap running. Canadians are among the highest water users in the world—according to Environment Canada, we use roughly twice as much per person as in other industrialized countries. Guilt can be a powerful motivation to change.

Scrape dishes clean

Good news for whoever's on dish duty tonight: no need to pre-rinse your dishes. Pre-rinsing not only wastes water, it doesn't improve cleaning results. So no need to run the tap—just scrape off extra food before items go into the dishwasher. (Be sure to scrape them well, though. Food waste builds up in the machine and reduces its efficiency, not to mention its effectiveness.) Be sure to regularly clean the filter at the bottom of your dishwasher to keep it running efficiently.

 ## Don't leave chemicals on the cutlery

The next question you have to ask yourself is, how clean are my dishes really getting if I'm using petroleum-derived detergent to clean them? As with all your other cleaning products, make sure your dishwasher soap is biodegradable and made of only vegetable-based surfactants. (See Chapters 3, 4 and 5 for more on natural cleaning alternatives.) Powdered soaps are lighter and so require less energy to ship. Powdered dishwasher soaps usually come in cardboard boxes, which require less energy to manufacture and can be more successfully recycled. Buying in bulk will save you money and save packaging.

My favourite dishwasher powders are made by Seventh Generation and Citradish. Both are available at health food stores, along with other natural brands.

If you want to be DIY about dish soap, mix equal parts borax and baking soda (for hard water, double the amount of baking soda) and store in a tightly sealed container. Use 2 tablespoons per load, and use vinegar instead of chemical rinse-aid products in the rinse cycle.

[3]
How to **Clean the Kitchen**

Let's face it, we've been hoodwinked—convinced by marketing geniuses that the only way to get that sparkle of sanitation and good hygiene is to wipe and spray every inch of our eating areas with toxic chemicals. What would our grandmothers say if they could see us spending our hard-earned dollars on liquid gel tablets, foaming spray and disposable cleaning wipes? They'd say that a few natural ingredients from the cupboard do just as good a job for mere pennies, and they'd be right.

Most of the chemicals used in household cleaning products were originally developed during World War II as part of warfare research. In a bizarre twist of logic, they were then applied to other uses, including domestic cleaning products and agricultural pesticides. It's hard to believe that before the 1940s, houses were kept clean using fairly simple and affordable stuff.

So put an end to paper towels and excessively packaged cleansers that nibble away at your grocery budget. Instead, spend that money on yummy food, and prepare it on clean counters that don't harbour dangerous ingredients.

Here are some squeaky clean strategies that keep my house healthy and hygienic—at least for five minutes until someone messes it up again.

#1 Ditch the toxic cleaning products

While they might not all bear a warning label, most of your household cleansers contain ingredients that are as dangerous for you as they are for the earth. And you thought that headache was from having to clean the bathroom. Research has shown that indoor air is 2 to 11 times more polluted than the air outside. The list of toxic chemicals floating around in your house right now is downright terrifying.

THE SCARE:

→ **Chlorine bleach:** Even short-term exposure can cause mild asthmatic symptoms or more serious respiratory problems.

→ **Ammonia:** Used in many window and glass cleaners, it is a serious eye irritant that can cause headaches and lung irritation.

→ **Nitrobenzene:** In furniture and floor polishes, it has been associated with skin discolouration, vomiting, cancer, birth defects and even death.

→ **Petroleum:** Many conventional detergents (surfactants), solvents and polishes contain paraffin, mineral oil, diethylene glycol, perchloroethylene or butyl cellosolve—all of which are derived from petroleum, a nonrenewable resource whose refining process causes major pollution.

→ **Phthalates:** While they make those perfume smells last longer, they are also linked to cancer and disease of the reproductive system in laboratory animals.

→ **Phosphates:** "Increase your cleaning power!" while encouraging algae growth in water systems, which damages other marine life.

→ **Antibacterial agents:** These can lead to an increase in antibiotic-resistant bacteria, those superbugs wreaking havoc in some hospitals recently.

Most of what you need to keep your house perfectly clean is already in your pantry. Here are your top 10 must-haves for natural cleaning:

Already got 'em: baking soda, distilled white vinegar, lemons, vodka, olive oil

Might need to shop for 'em: liquid Castile soap, borax, empty spray bottles, washing soda, tea tree oil

Baking soda is an excellent abrasive cleanser for sinks and pots; white vinegar and hot water make an instant floor cleaner; olive oil is a beauty for polishing wood furniture and floors; tea tree oil is a natural disinfectant. See below for all the wonderful cleaning solutions you can make.

Clean sinks and counters naturally

Our obsession with disinfectants is tending toward paranoia. In a twist of irony, scientists are concerned that the increase in use of antibacterial and antimicrobial disinfectants is actually contributing to the surge of resistant bacteria, or superbugs. Many of the ingredients in those antimicrobial products are actually pesticides.

The simplest way to clean your sink? Just sprinkle baking soda and rub with a damp cloth using a little elbow grease.

For counters, try using a few drops of mild dish soap on a damp microfibre cloth. Rinse and rewipe if you used too much soap and see any residue on the counter. This is the best method for cleaning stainless steel too. Some great natural dish soaps are made by Seventh Generation and Ecover. Nature Clean, Simply Clean, Attitude and Eco-Max are very good Canadian-made products. These companies also make excellent all-purpose cleaning sprays.

I get my kids to wipe off the table after dinner each night, so I wanted something they could spritz and spray with abandon without worrying about anything getting into their little eyes or lungs. I fill a spray bottle nearly full with water, and then add 10 drops each of tea tree oil and lavender oil. It's naturally antiseptic and antifungal, with a great smell too. And our table is clean as a whistle.

#3 Clean glass and surfaces naturally

Club soda is an excellent window cleaner, so a spray bottle of that can tackle your mirrors and glass surfaces too (see Chapter 6, "How to Wash the Windows"). Seventh Generation and Eco-Max make scented or unscented spray cleaners—no streaks and no toxins.

#4 Clean floors naturally

Everybody loves a sparkly clean kitchen floor, but nobody needs the headaches, or childhood asthma, caused by the volatile organic compounds (VOCs) found in most floor waxes and polishes. For a clean floor without the headaches, use a broom. Daily sweeping—three times a day if my four-year-old is visiting you—will keep a han-

---

STAR CLEANING POWER If you loved him in *St. Elsewhere*, you'll love him even more now. Ed Begley, Jr., has thrown his celebrity status behind the green movement for decades, and now the world seems finally ready for a guy who powers his toaster by riding a stationary bike. Ed's TV show *Living with Ed* (which airs on HGTV in Canada) follows the actor living green for life every day. His line of cleaning products is the first to be C2C (cradle to cradle) certified—meaning the planet has been taken into consideration during the entire manufacturing process. Begley's Best cleaning products biodegrade within three to seven days. Check out www.begleysbest.com.

dle on dirt and grit that can mark and scuff the floor when left underfoot.

An exciting revolution in domestic sanitation is the microfibre mop. As with a lot of new technology, a microfibre mop is not cheap, but it will of course save you money on soap, as it requires only plain water to wash your floor.

To wash with a regular mop, simply add ½ cup white vinegar to 4 litres hot water. For a stronger cleanser, mix ¼ cup washing soda, 1 tablespoon liquid Castile soap, ¼ cup vinegar and 8 litres hot water, stirring to dissolve the washing soda. For wood floors, mix ¼ cup liquid Castile soap, 1 cup vinegar and 8 litres warm water. To polish wood floors, mix equal parts vinegar, olive oil and vodka, or simply rub with olive oil.

SWIFT MOP CONVERSION
If you're using one of those spray-and-wipe floor mops with disposable pads, stop and think of all the money you are spending on refills of the cleaning spray and packages of disposable mop pads. And what about the toxic ingredients in those spray refills? You can't even refill the bottle with natural ingredients—I tried without success. So, why not just keep the handle, put an old washcloth underneath it, and stick it to the Mop Man?

#5 Wipe and scrub with nature

Nylon sponges are derived from petroleum, which means they are not recyclable or biodegradable. So even when you think its life is over, that Muppet-green sponge will live forever in a landfill after you've thrown it out. You can reduce the waste, and conserve the energy required to create that nylon, by using natural scrubbing options. Cellulose sponges are biodegradable and actually soak up spills more quickly, as they are more naturally absorbent, and natural sea sponges can be found at most natural food stores. Microfibre cloths are widely available and are the best option for cleaning stainless steel. Mabu cloths are popular at my house. Made from vegetable cellulose pulp, they are naturally bacteria resistant, and they provide the thickest, softest all-purpose wipe-up I've ever seen. Washcloths can be tossed in with the laundry for cleaning; natural sponges or wooden scrub brushes with natural bristles can be soaked in boiling water for three to five minutes to disinfect.

#6 Buy bar soap, not the pump

Replace that plastic soap dispenser beside your sink with a bar of glycerine or other biodegradable soap. There are about a million different kinds of natural soap bars on the market these days, sold everywhere from grocery stores to gift shops. They are cheaper and longer lasting, and of course they require no packaging. And you don't have to turn them upside down for the last three days of use to get the tail end of the soap out. Those dispenser pumps drive me nuts.

WHAT'S IN YOUR SOAP? In the last several years, it seems antibacterial soaps have become the new standard for handwashing—which goes to show you the power of fear over reason. While handwashing is recommended as the single best way to avoid germs, the American Medical Association has stated that antibacterial soaps have no more benefit than ordinary soaps. Which is a shame, really, because that means all the buildup of antibacterial and antifungal agents, like triclosan and triclocarban, in natural water systems is for nothing. Research at the Johns Hopkins Bloomberg School of Public Health has determined that these two chemicals, found in many household soaps, toothpastes and deodorants, create carcinogenic dioxins when exposed to sunlight. Researchers at Virginia Polytechnic Institute have also found that triclosan and triclocarban react with chlorinated drinking water to produce dangerously high levels of chloroform in the water—chloroform is listed as a probable human carcinogen, and has been linked with miscarriages and bladder cancer.

The American Medical Association has been advocating since 2000 for the U.S. Food and Drug Administration (FDA) to review regulations around household use of these chemicals. Take matters into your own hands—avoid products listing triclosan or triclocarban as ingredients.

[4]
How to **Remove Stains**

As a mother of three young boys, I have had my fair share of experience with stains and spills. Actually, I'm pretty much an expert. Just name a surface or fabric, and chances are it's been spilled on at my house. But I am careful to attack every spill with the health of the planet—and the household—in mind. In our fury to eradicate stains from our lives in our "whiter than white" culture, we've created something of a toxic soup in the average North American household. Ample research shows that we are polluting the air inside our homes with all the deeply toxic commercial stain-removing products we use. So what's in them?

THE SCARE:
→ **Ammonia:** A suspected carcinogen, it is highly corrosive and can burn or irritate the skin. Overexposure could lead to kidney failure.

→ **Bleach:** It can create highly toxic and deadly chlorine gas if mixed with acid-based cleaning products, which is easy enough to do if you're using a variety of commercial bathroom-cleaning products. In case you forgot, chlorine gas was used as a weapon in World War I.

→ **Petroleum-based surfactants:** Often made from coal tar, a known carcinogen, the products containing them may be cancer causing. They are also fat

33

soluble, so they wind up in our fat stores long after we've finished cleaning the rug.

→ **Petrochemicals:** Usually found in spot and stain removers, dandies like toluene and xylene cause reproductive damage, and perchloroethylene is a known carcinogen.

By contrast, here is the decidedly non-scary arsenal of stain removers, most of which are probably already in your fridge or pantry, to keep your house clean and green: baking soda, vinegar, lemon, milk, club soda, corn-starch, unseasoned meat tenderizer and salt. I call them the gentle giants.

Here's your non-toxic stain-removal shopping list (stuff you may not already have kicking around): Castile soap, borax, distilled white vinegar, glycerine, rubbing alcohol, 3 percent hydrogen peroxide, washing soda, biodegradable liquid dish soap. And don't forget the spray bottles. Everything else, you've probably already got in the kitchen.

The only stains I haven't been able to get out using these safe, non-toxic and biodegradable alternatives are the ones that happened when I wasn't looking and didn't discover until they'd already set in. The single best course of action on stain removal is to get to it the moment it happens. Having said that, one product that is remark-ably forgiving about the amount of time passed since the stain set is called Pink Solution. Made by Vancouver-based Earthcare, Pink Solution is a non-toxic, organic

GENIUS IN A BOTTLE **Your best bet when you overhaul your cleaning cupboard is to get yourself a few empty spray bottles. Fill them up with these safe and sure recipes, then label them clearly. If you're anything like me, you'll need to use them again before too long.**

and biodegradable product made from natural enzymes. It's kind of like algae eating your ugly spills for dinner. While devotees rave on the Pink Solution website about its myriad uses, from laundry to dishwashing, my personal favourite is how it munches up old carpet stains as if they happened just moments ago. Check out www.pinksolution.ca for more information.

#1 General spot remover

Dissolve ¼ cup borax in hot water. Let cool. Keep on hand in a resealable container. Apply directly to stains on fabrics or carpets, using a sponge, a Q-tip or a spray bottle, depending on the size of the spot.

#2 General carpet stain removal

Fill one of your trusty 500 millilitre spray bottles half full with warm water. Fill the rest of the bottle with vinegar, almost to top. Add 1 tablespoon liquid Castile soap. Spray on carpet stain until soaked. Blot with a damp cloth.

#3 The motherload carpet stain removal

Mix a ¼ cup each of salt, borax and vinegar. Rub the paste into your carpet and leave it for a few hours. Vacuum. Tell yourself they'll be grown up soon enough and you'll miss their carefree, careless years.

Another great thing about using cleaning ingredients that you can also use to make dinner is that your kids can safely and easily be included in the cleaning process. The best way to get them to take more care is to have them understand that objects have value, and to experience the effort that is required to keep them clean. (*Note: While borax is a naturally occurring mineral that is water soluble, it may cause irritation if inhaled. Use caution when dispensing the borax powder.*)

Red wine

It's one of Murphy's lesser-known laws: for every occasion that includes red wine there is an equal and obvious spill that is usually executed by and/or upon the individual wearing white.

Immediately cover stain with salt or soda water, then soak in milk before washing. Also see #5a, below.

 ## Grease

a. *On cotton:* Spread fabric over a bowl or another opening to allow water to pass through it, rather than soaking it. Then pour boiling water through it, followed by baking soda. (This also worked brilliantly for a red wine spill on a white slipcover one Christmas Eve.)

b. *On fabrics other than cotton:* Blot with a clean towel, dampen stain with water and rub with soap and baking soda. Wash in hot water.

 ## Blood

When blood is shed, warm water is dread. Just think of Truman Capote's 1965 blockbuster crime novel, *In Cold Blood*. Soak stain immediately in cold water, mixed with a handful of salt. If the stain persists, mix cornstarch, cornmeal and water to form a loose paste, and then apply the mixture directly to the stain. Allow to dry, and brush away.

For old blood stains that have set, try covering with a paste of meat tenderizer and warm water. Leave for 20 minutes, then wash in cold water.

 ## Berry juice

Pour boiling water over fabric (see #5a, above). If you are worried about a delicate fabric, treat the spot with fresh lemon juice. For tougher, set stains, blot with glycerine and let sit for 30 minutes. Rinse with warm water and hang to dry.

For berry juice spills on carpet, blot any excess liquid or berry with a clean, dry towel. Spray with a mixture of equal parts vinegar and water; blot dry. Dab and rub gently with mild laundry soap and water; blot dry. Wipe with cold water, then blot dry with a clean towel.

 ## #8 Lipstick

Rub with vegetable shortening and wash with washing soda (sodium carbonate).

 ## #9 Ink

Soak stain in milk. Dip a Q-tip in a small amount of hydrogen peroxide and dab onto stain. Most ink dissolves in alcohol, so you can also soak the stain in rubbing alcohol. Make sure you place a towel underneath the garment to absorb the ink as it dissolves. Ink on walls can be removed with rubbing alcohol on a damp cloth.

 ## #10 Rust

Saturate with sour milk (adding 2 teaspoons of vinegar to milk makes it sour) or lemon juice, and rub with salt. Place in direct sunlight until dry, then wash.

#11 Perspiration

Pink Solution (see pages 34–35) works wonders on embarrassing underarm stains on those favourite summer T-shirts. The enzymes actually eat up the bacteria causing the stain. It's like a science experiment that works in your favour. If you don't have Pink Solution on hand yet, soak the item in a mixture of warm water and vinegar.

Coffee

Mix a raw egg yolk with lukewarm water and rub on stain.

Now, since you're usually wearing that fabulous shirt when you dribble your coffee down your front, you may not be able to slather it in egg yolk right away—so the stain may be set by the time you get around to tackling it. Try the boiling water method described in #5a, sprinkling a little borax onto the stain before you pour the water through it.

 ## Porcelain stains

Combine borax and lemon juice into a paste. Let sit on the stain for two hours, then scrub object.

 ## Gum

Rub with ice, until gum flakes off surface.

Recap on the basic rules of non-toxic stain removal:
Act fast and have patience. Where a commercial product may give you a quick fix ("Spray it on and forget about your troubles!"), the natural route offers long-term gain. Take a few extra minutes to soak, gently scrub or work away at your stain, and you'll be healthier for it. And just as clean.

Other things to remember:
Sunshine will whiten cotton and linen, free of charge.

When you are buying furniture, don't go for the stain proofing. Scotchgard and other stain-resistant treatments use toxic chemicals, including formaldehyde (which is, let's not forget, used in the process of embalming dead people) and perfluorochemicals such as PFOAs, which the EPA calls toxic "to an extraordinary degree." This is what you and the people you love will be sitting, lying and possibly even jumping on, absorbing directly into your respiratory tract and bloodstream. Now that you've got a toolkit for tackling stains naturally, you can skip the chemical bath. See Chapter 10, "How to Decorate Your House," for more non-toxic furniture suggestions.

[5]
How to **Do Laundry**

As much as we'd all like to get out of laundry duty—to padlock the washer and dryer and put up a sign, "Laundry facilities closed to save energy: please use deodorant regularly and keep spills to a minimum"—it's just not going to happen. But the amount of energy used in your laundry room is staggering: your dryer is the second biggest user of electricity in your house, after your fridge, which is on all the time.

Fortunately, you can do lots of green for life things to lighten your load on the earth, if not on your laundry basket.

#1 High-efficiency washer

If you're in the market for a new washing machine, be sure to invest in a front-loading model. (If your old machines are post-1997 models and they're working fine, don't send them to a landfill just yet. The greener choice is to use them wisely until they wear out. Read on for lots of ways to make your existing appliances more eco-friendly.) Front-loading washing machines cost slightly more than the old top-loading kind, significantly more than buying a second-hand top-loader, to be sure. But if you employ long-term thinking, and possibly get a deal on a longer-term payment plan, you'll see the benefit of the front-loading model.

First of all, its capacity is significantly higher, so you can wash more clothes (and bedding and sleeping bags and stinky hockey gear …) at a time. Which means fewer trips down the basement stairs for you, and less electricity to pay for. Front-loading machines use half the energy of top-loaders, and nearly half the amount of water. An Energy Star model will save you roughly $100 every year on your hydro bill.

Better still is how dry your clothes feel when they come out of the washer. Front-loaders spin the clothes so effectively, they need way less time in the dryer.

 ## #2 High-efficiency dryer

The same story goes for the front-loading dryer—it has a bigger capacity and significantly lower energy cost. Having said that, don't buy a bigger model than your family needs. Look for the model with the lowest EnerGuide score that is big enough for your average load (EnerGuide is a government initiative that rates appliances for efficiency to help consumers make the best environmental choices—see http://oee.nrcan.gc.ca/energuide/index.cfm). Most new dryer models also feature a moisture sensor so you won't waste energy overdrying your clothes.

#3 Other drying tricks

Of course, the best way to reduce the energy use from your dryer is to not use your dryer! I know that sounds heretical, but when you think about it, throwing clothes into the dryer is a nothing more than a habit. A darn convenient one, I concede, especially when you're busy. But the dryer takes a real toll on your energy bills, and on your clothing, too. Whenever there's time, hang-dry whatever you can. Many synthetic garments (think workout gear and fleece stuff) actually say "hang to dry" right on their label—they will certainly last longer and hold their shape better if kept out of the heat of the dryer. An outdoor clothesline is ideal and oh so European, but in this country, a great all-season hang-dry option is a collapsible drying rack. It folds up and tucks away in your presumably cramped laundry quarters, then opens up to hang all manner of clothing to dry overnight. And as they dry, your wet clothes will add a little moisture to the dry air in your house through the long Canadian winter.

For stuff that absolutely has to go in the dryer, be sure to use the moisture sensor. Don't just spin that wheel without thinking and let the dryer bake your clothes. Overdrying is as hard on your clothes as it is on your pocketbook. Try using the permanent press setting, which will run a cool-down for the last few minutes of the cycle, so the air keeps blowing through your clothes but without that high-energy heat. Use the timer on the dryer, and set it for as low as 30 minutes. Let the dryer do the heavy lifting on water removal, then pull out your trusty hanging rack to get the last bit done.

Hanging to dry will help you avoid the dreaded static cling as well. If you do need a fabric softener, skip the coal-tar dyes and chemical perfumes found in most products, and add ½ cup white vinegar, baking soda or borax to your rinse cycle. Or throw a ball of aluminium foil in the dryer to reduce static cling naturally.

You may already know this from household fire-safety training, but a clogged lint trap is a fire hazard. Ever hear of people whose houses burned down while they went out and left the dryer running? Bet they all had a backlog of lint stuck in their mesh trap. Empty your lint trap every single time you put in a new load. A lint-filled trap also means your dryer has to work harder to get the clothes dry, which can add up to about 30 percent more in energy costs.

#4 ## Natural laundry soaps and detergents

Some of the most harsh and nasty household chemicals are found right in your laundry room—and therefore all over the fabrics that you and your loved ones come into contact with as you eat, sleep and play.

Many commercial laundry detergents are petroleum based, which means not only are they using up a non-renewable resource, but they create pollution just to manufacture, they create more pollution when they don't break down completely in the water system, and they are harsh on your skin to boot.

Now you may be one of those people who have come to associate that perfumed laundry smell with cleanliness. I have a dear friend who feels that her clothes just aren't clean if they don't reek of sickly sweet perfumes from scented soaps and fabric softeners. I'm telling you, I can smell her kids coming from the other side of the park. And when one of my sons borrowed her son's T-shirt and I laundered it before giving it back, my entire load of wash smelled like her fabric softener—just from putting one T-shirt into the mix! Now that's industrial-strength perfume at work.

That strong smell that marketers have brainwashed us into believing equals clean clothes is nothing more than a toxic chemical cocktail: any number of synthetic ingredients are used to create your favourite "fresh clean" fragrance. Synthetic fragrances are known to trigger asthma attacks and are common skin irritants. The *Guide to Less Toxic Products* cites clinical observations showing that exposure to fragrances can cause depression, hyperactivity and irritability.

Feeling clean yet? Me neither.

No, the approach to clean clothes in my house is based on the old-fashioned wisdom contained in the following pages—which is often a cheaper approach, too—and on some alternative cleaning products that I can recommend thoroughly.

Soapworks Pure Laundry Soap Powder with borax is the one I swear by. Made in Canada and sold with minimal packaging, either in bulk or in a paper bag, it works like a dream and contains no harsh chemicals. The Soapworks natural laundry bar is also great to have on hand for rubbing on stains. Ecover stain remover has a handy scrubber on the spout for those ground-in stains. But the best commercial product for stain removal (see Chapter 4, "How to Remove Stains," for homemade stain removal recipes) is Nature Clean's laundry stain remover. Made from nothing but corn and castor plant oil, it works miracles. For overall brightening of your whites, look for Ecover's chlorine-free laundry bleach, which is 100 percent percarbonate (basically salt, limestone and oxygenated water) and has recycled cardboard packaging. You don't have to wear dingy grey whites to be earth friendly. Other natural brands to look for are Seventh Generation and Soap Factory, which, like Nature Clean, is made in Canada. All these products are petroleum, chlorine and phosphate free, biodegrade quickly, and are safe for septic systems.

PHOSPHATES ARE JUST THE BEGINNING Don't feel too virtuous for using phosphate-free laundry detergent: phosphates are no longer permitted in any laundry detergents because of the severe damage they inflict on aquatic wildlife by causing algae blooms. So that claim on the label isn't enough to make your soap green for life. Make sure your laundry soap is made using plant-based surfactants, is non-petroleum derived and is fragrance free.

#5 Natural whitening

It's hard to believe that we have evolved to a place where we care so much about "whiter-than-white whites" that we are willing to keep deadly chemicals in our household cupboards. Stop the insanity: cut out chlorine bleach! Sodium hypochlorite is a corrosive chemical that can be fatal if swallowed. It's the reason parents of small children invest heavily in military-strength locks and bolts for undercounter cupboards. An eye, skin and respiratory irritant, and a possible neurotoxin, bleach is scary stuff.

Look for a non-chlorine bleach. Hydrogen peroxide is a powerful whitening bleach that uses oxygen to whiten instead of dioxin-causing chlorine. Antiviral, anti-bacterial and antifungal, hydrogen peroxide has lots of household uses, and it's safe for the environment.

If you can't believe your laundry soap will get clothes clean enough in cold water (wash all your clothes in cold water—see below), add borax to your arsenal. Borax is a must-have item in every green for life household. Add about ½ cup to any load to presoak stains, and have whites come out whiter. Borax is also a detergent booster, so it will cut your use of laundry soap in half.

#6 Other washing tricks and a story about my mother

With characteristic devotion and selflessness, my mother did my brother's laundry for years (years!), even after he'd moved out of the house. She always said it was too tricky for him to know what colours to wash at what temperature. (Which we all know had more to do with a loving mum than an incapable youngest son.)

But boys growing up in this day and age don't have such an excuse for opting out of learning to wash their own laundry. Cold water washing is the way to go. You don't pay to heat hot water for laundry, and you never have to see your favourite white blouse turn pink when someone throws their new red boxer shorts into the whites load. The dial on our machine at home never moves off "cold wash, cold rinse." (So my nine-year-old is working on other excuses to shirk the chore.) The other dial that never moves on our machine is load size: it's always full.

Yes, there's more good news for the lazy launderer: washing machines are at their most energy efficient when they are fully loaded. (Not stuffed to the gills so the agitator can't spin properly, mind you. Don't pack the clothes in, just place them in loosely.) So unless you have enough dirty stuff to fill the drum, take a pass on doing the wash.

And another trick from my mother, ever the frugal war baby: you don't need to use as much laundry detergent as the manufacturer recommends. ("Sweetie, they just want you to use lots of the stuff so you'll run out to buy more.") Use about half the amount of detergent suggested on the package, even with the eco-friendly brands.

Eighteen minutes of scrubbing your wash? Why waste the energy? Set your machine to the shortest wash time possible. Bet you won't notice a bit of difference in your clothes.

Clean your machine about once a year to keep it working well and lengthen its lifespan. Pour 2 cups distilled white vinegar into the washing machine on its own and run a full cycle.

#7 Ironing tricks

I'll admit that my favourite ironing trick is to avoid having to plug one in at all: fold clothes as soon as they come out of the dryer to prevent wrinkling.

To avoid the formaldehyde and other chemicals in

commercial starching agents, make your own instead. Mix 2 tablespoons cornstarch with 3 cups water, and pour into a spray bottle for natural spray starch.

To maintain your iron, clean it with a paste of baking soda and warm water, rubbing with a soft, damp cloth. If your iron sticks or develops residue on the ironing surface, sprinkle table salt onto a piece of white paper and iron over it until the iron runs smoothly again.

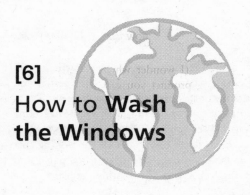

[6]
How to **Wash the Windows**

It's an annual chore that no one looks forward to. But nothing takes the spring out of springtime more than noticing all the grimy buildup on your windows as that welcome post-winter sunshine begins to pour through them.

The only thing less appealing than actually cleaning the windows is thinking about what all those toxic chemicals being spritzed onto your panes—and into your lungs—might be doing to you.

THE SCARE:
Butyl cellosolve causes nerve damage, **ammonia** irritates lung and eye tissue, and **perfumes**, while they may mask the harsh odours of some of their fellow chemicals, can cause nerve damage and cancer. And that **blue dye**? Well, you know that's not derived from plant material now is it?

But you don't have to inhale danger when you do tackle the big job. Using completely safe ingredients and with a handy bit of R&R—that is, reusing and recycling—you can have squeaky clean windows without the headache.

#1 Cleaning fluids

Remember when those apple farmers swore their pesticides were so safe they could drink them, and they

48

did, just to prove it? (I wonder where they are now.) This is one cleaning product you can definitely drink straight from the bottle and live to tell the tale. Club soda is the best choice for window washing. Just fill a spray bottle with regular club soda, spray it on and wipe off with a dry rag.

Another choice is our old pal distilled white vinegar in water (1 tablespoon to 1 litre of warm water), which you can also drink, though it won't taste as good.

If you've been less than diligent about regular window washings, you may need more than a spritz or two of liquid to tackle the buildup. Cornstarch mixed with warm water (½ cup cornstarch to 2 to 3 litres of warm water) is another excellent and potable option, which can be applied with a sponge or an old towel and as much elbow grease as required.

#2 Drying cloths

Here's where the reusing and recycling comes in. The best drying material for squeaky clean windows, one that leaves no bits of lint or dust on the glass surface, is newspaper. Yes, the daily rag beats a cloth rag 10 times out of 10. The porous newsprint soaks up every bit of liquid, and the ink seems to lift the dirt right off. Just scrunch them up in your hand and wipe while the surface is still damp. Then put them back into the recycling box and let the sun shine in.

[7]
How to Unclog a Drain

There's no question, a backed-up sink is a problem in need of an immediate solution. But before you bring out the skulls and crossbones, remember that drain cleaners may be fatal if ingested.

 ## #1 Unclog naturally

This little trick works just as well, is non-toxic and won't kill any aquatic life when it leaves your pipe. It's like a chemistry class in your kitchen, so it's kind of fun too!

Pour ¼ cup baking soda and ¼ cup salt down the drain.

Add ½ cup vinegar and insert the plug or sink stopper.

Plug in the kettle.

Check your phone messages, or find some other equally satisfying use of a precious quarter hour of your time.

After 15 minutes, pour boiling water down the drain.

Breathe easy. Problem solved.

#2 Give it the snake attack

The mechanical snake has long been the plumber's best friend. For about $10 at your local hardware store, you can have a snake as a friend too. It works pretty much how you'd expect: the "head" of the snake has prongs on it that will grab hold of whatever gunk is blocking your pipes. Insert the head down the overflow opening of a bathroom sink or tub, or straight down the drain of the kitchen sink. Crank the snake for a couple of minutes until you feel contact with the perpetrator. Then listen up for that sweet sound you've been waiting for—the slurping suck of a newly opened passage. Voilà! A chemical-free way to restore the flow.

#3 Stop clogs before they happen

Leave the stopper for your kitchen sink over the drain in the unlocked position whenever you are working at the sink. This will collect any bits of food or packaging that might slip down the drain and build up to a clog. Empty it regularly to avoid any extra bacterial growth in your sink.

Some people swear by the hair screens for shower drains. Metal or wire mesh discs with a fairly loose weave, they start to look like Cousin It from the Addams family after a while, at which point you can easily lift them out and empty all that shed hair into the garbage pail.

[8]
How to Unclog a Toilet

This one's easy. Three simple steps. It goes like this:

Step 1: Buy a plunger.

Step 2: Stick the bulbous end in your clogged toilet.

Step 3: Push down on the handle end a bunch of times, until you see the water level in the toilet going down. Remove the plunger, and attempt a flush if it looks like the coast is clear. If not, repeat steps two and three.

In most cases, that's all you'll ever need to unclog the situation. That's right, no chemicals required. And a new plunger costs less than $10.

Now, if my four-year-old is visiting you, and he's been up to his old tricks—which is to say, anything from your cell phone to the kitchen flashlight has been sent on a whitewater adventure through the household plumbing—no amount of plunging will help you. For that kind of clog, you graduate to Full Toilet Bowl Removal. Now I never thought I'd say this, but taking apart a toilet is really not all that hard. Okay, I also have the plumber on speed dial, but it is possible to do it without him. Having three boys has forced me to learn all kinds of new skills, including patience. And toilet bowl removal. Check out **www.doityourself.com** for the nitty gritty.

[9]
How to **Renovate Your House**

Only in a nest-obsessed culture like ours could a tall man in construction coveralls become a mega-celebrity, based largely on his considerable skill with a power saw. Yes, we do love Mike Holmes because we do love to renovate—and if we can't do it ourselves right now, well, we'll just watch other people do it on TV.

Traditionally, most folks renovate a home to make it bigger or maybe a little fancier. But these days, home renovating is about a lot more than space and image. Making your home more energy efficient is all the renovation rage these days—good for the earth, good for your pocketbook. If you're looking to justify a little renovating of your own, there's never been a better time. The 13 million homes in Canada are contributing hugely to the country's greenhouse gas emissions, and the government says it will pay you up to $5000 to make yours more energy efficient. And the market will thank you for it when it comes time to sell: a recent eco-home survey by a leading real estate company found that 72 percent of Canadians will look for green improvements in their next home purchase. Most of those said they are willing to pay up to $20,000 more for a home with green features. So get out those coveralls and start greening your investment.

#1 Furnace

If you are planning to spend any money to fix up your house, the furnace is the smartest place to start. I know it's tucked away in the basement, so no one can see where you spent the small fortune for a new one. But a furnace that is more than 20 years old really needs to be replaced. A new furnace is a big investment, but the difference it will make to your monthly heating bills will help offset the cost. Look for an Energy Star high-efficiency furnace, ideally around 90 percent efficiency. The percentage refers to how much of the fuel source is actually converted into heat. Lower-efficiency models send a lot of that expensive fuel out your chimney—so your money is literally going up in smoke. A dual-speed fan on the furnace means the unit will use less energy when there's less demand for heat.

Even an Energy Star needs a strong supporting cast—be sure to replace your furnace filter once a month during the winter and have your ducts cleaned regularly. In older houses a duct cleaning should include an inspection to see that no sections have become dislodged—if one of your vents doesn't seem to be delivering much air to the room, that could be why.

PROGRAMMED FOR SAVINGS Let's take that high-efficiency dual-speed fan furnace up another eco-notch. Why pay for heating or cooling when no one is home? Or when everyone is asleep under cozy blankets? Spend $50 to $100 on a programmable thermostat—it will pay for itself after just one winter. Program it to suit your family's schedule, with separate settings for weekdays and weekends. For every degree you lower the temperature (or raise it in the summer), you save 2 percent on your energy costs.

#2 ## Caulk and weatherstripping

Maybe a new furnace just isn't in the budget this year. If you want to start saving money to buy a new furnace, what better way than to keep all that expensive heat inside your house? You can do that easily with a couple of tubes of caulk and some weatherstripping, which will go easy on your wallet and tough on your drafts. Weatherstripping is the roll of sticky-backed foam that fits neatly along door and window seams, blocking any air leaks; caulk is for patching any cracks or leaks in window frames and baseboards. To avoid the off-gassing of solvents in latex or oil-based products, look for 100 percent silicone caulk at the hardware store, available in clear or white. Or you can order non-toxic, water-based AFM Safecoat caulk through the Ottawa-based Healthiest Home store (www.thehealthiesthome.com).

Okay, you've got the gear, now where do you start? Grab your caulk and a stick of incense and I'll show you a productive way to spend a free afternoon. Walk through your house with the lit incense stick on a day when there is a little wind. Holding the incense stick near your windows, doors and baseboards allows you to *see* the drafts—when the incense smoke wafts in the breeze, that's your money you're looking at floating away in lost heat. Draftproofing will lower your heating bills by roughly 20 percent.

Now maybe you like the sound of the savings, but like most of us, you can't find the spare afternoon to caulk. For those of you with better intentions than execution, there's likely a home energy audit company in your area that can do the draftproofing (and the insulating, see below) for you (check out Ontario's Enwise Power Solutions at www.enwisepower.com or B.C.'s Home Performance at www.homeperformance.com). Many provincial governments offer rebates for improvements to your home's efficiency based on an energy audit.

#3 Insulation

"Resale value" is the watchword in home renovations. And with the cost of fuel climbing ever higher, smart home shoppers are doing their research and asking to see energy bills. No matter how gorgeous your home looks, if you can't keep it warm in the winter and cool in the summer, nobody is going to want to live there.

Insulation is like a sweater for your house. You wouldn't send your child outside in the winter without a sweater, so don't do it to your home. Your choice of insulation will depend on the age of your home and what it's made with. (During a home renovation show I worked on for the CBC, a Halifax homeowner discovered her postwar house had been insulated with—wait for it— seaweed.) For houses with exterior clapboard or siding, blown cellulose is the best option. Made from recycled newspapers or wood pulp by-product, cellulose can be blown into the cavity between the drywall and the exterior siding. You'll feel the difference immediately, both in warmth and in soundproofing. If you're renovating down to the studs, fibreglass batting goes in between the joists—a job that is easy to do yourself.

However, fibreglass can release airborne pollutants that irritate lungs and stimulate migraines, so it should be carefully sealed with an airtight barrier overtop. That vapour barrier is also important as it keeps moisture from the house out of the insulation and walls. Spray-on polyurethane is commonly used for insulating, especially in hard-to-reach floor cavities or attics, but you should know that that expanding blue foam leaches brominated flame retardants, which have been confirmed toxic in animal tests.

If marinated tofu has never been your thing, why don't you order your soy product in the foam form? Heat Lok Soya is spray foam insulation made from soybean and other vegetable oils and recycled plastic bottles. It provides effective non-toxic warmth—no marinating required. Check out www.foamcomfort.ca for more information.

#4 Windows

We crave that brightness through the Canadian winter, but we don't want more heat indoors during a Canadian July. Spending a bit more on quality energy-efficient windows will save you money on heating and cooling in the not so long run. The bells and whistles to ask for at the window store are triple pane with argon gas (multiple panes of glass keep indoor and outdoor temperatures from colliding, and the inert gas in between each pane is even more of a buffer); double-glazed low-E (emissivity) coated Energy Star glass (the panes are treated with an invisible oxide coating for even better insulation, to further discourage the glass from transferring heat from the indoors out, or vice versa).

If you want to feel positively futuristic in your choice of windows, how about glass that insulates like a wall? Toronto-based Eco Insulating Glass makes windows coated with a film of invisible nanoparticles that block out exterior temperature, infrared light and most of the UV rays. Check out www.ecoglass.ca.

> STEP AWAY FROM THE ASBESTOS **Houses built before the 1970s may well contain asbestos, a hazardous mineral fibre that is linked to abdominal cancer and lung disease. It is often found in the insulation around pipes, ducts and boilers; in old vinyl floor tile; or in drywall joint compound.** *If you suspect there may be asbestos in your home, do not remove it.* **Dislodging asbestos can release toxins into the air, so it's best left untouched. Simply box it in or call professionals to remove it.**

If nanoparticles aren't in your budget, any covering over a window will be a bit of a barrier to heat loss—closing curtains and even hanging blankets are decidedly low-tech options, but both can improve a window draft. Cellular blinds for windows or skylights have a hollow honeycomb shape that acts as a barrier to prevent heat transfer.

If you're building from scratch or putting in new ones, remember that positioning windows to maximize daylight will reduce your need to turn on electric lights.

 ## #5 Air conditioning

If we're not paying to stay warm, we're paying to stay cool. But in view of how much of a strain air conditioning puts on the electrical grid and how much greenhouse gas ensues, it's cool not to be too cool. If you need a sweater in your house on a hot summer day, you're being gluttonous with your air conditioning.

In fact, maybe you don't need air conditioning at all. At our house, we use ceiling fans instead, and they use very little energy, especially the newer models. You can reset them to turn the other way in winter to help circulate heat and reduce your energy costs even further. Closing west-facing curtains during the afternoon keeps much of that beating hot sun out of your living space; opening windows to create a cross-draft allows for a bit of breeze most of the time.

If you're set on using air conditioning, be sure to install an Energy Star model. You'll see major savings when you buy Energy Star appliances—provincial rebates are just the beginning.

Another great solution for staying cool in the summer is to put a green roof on your house. Before you turn the page in a fit of anti-gardening anxiety, with visions of lugging your push mower up the attic stairs, hear me out.

We're not talking about having another garden to maintain. A green roof is the smartest way to lengthen the lifetime of your roof and improve your home's insulation all at once. Covered with hardy, drought-tolerant native grasses, your roof basically perspires out the heat from your house in the summer and has an extra layer of insulating protection through the winter. You'll be doing your bit for urban cooling too, with one less black roof cranking up city temperatures in summer. Check out www.eltgreenroofs.com for more information.

#6 Solar panels

We spend untold fortunes on air conditioning and sunscreen to keep those hot sun rays at bay. So what about putting the biggest star in the sky to work for us? Photovoltaic solar panels are popping up on more and more rooftops these days, and for good reason—they convert the sun's energy into electricity to power your home for free. And if you live in Ontario, you can actually sell that solar power back to your utility company to help pay for the cost of the panels. In 2006, Ontario created the Standard Offer Program allowing small renewable energy providers (that's you, with panels on the roof of your house) to sell any extra energy back to the

SOLAR ON THE SIDE Where photovoltaic panels on the rooftop turn sunlight into electricity, solar thermal panels are attached to the side of your house to maximize the heat of the sun and, in turn, heat your house. With no need to connect to the grid, solar thermal panels are much more affordable and easier to install, and they provide an immediate return on your investment. Check out the Canadian company Your Solar Home at www.yoursolarhome.com.

province at a fixed cost. The Worldwatch Institute has called this a historic move and a model for all of North America to follow.

To help bring down the price, why not shop in bulk? Some solar providers offer discounted installation if you can get a big enough group together in one neighbourhood. Check out www.ourpower.ca for inspiration on how to make it happen in your community.

 ## #7 Hot water tanks

If solar electricity is out of your price range, you can still harness the sun in your favour. A solar hot water tank costs considerably less than a full set of photovoltaic panels and, since water heating is responsible for nearly a quarter of your energy bills, you'll start saving money right away. You don't have to worry about cold showers—the technology is sound, so the only difference you'll notice is on your monthly heating bill.

An even less expensive energy upgrade is to go tankless. Traditional tank systems store water so that it is

---

TANK TIPS There are lots of easy and affordable ways to make your existing hot water tank more efficient. If you have an older model, it will need a tank blanket, a thick fibreglass wrap secured with waterproof tape that helps keep all that heat in the tank where it belongs. Turning down the thermostat on the unit—54 degrees Celsius is the recommended temperature—will keep the water hot enough to kill bacteria and still save energy. And when you're out of the house for more than a day or two, turn the temperature down even further. Most gas water heaters have a vacation setting (marked "VAC"); for other models, just turn it way down without turning it off. Who wants to pay to keep water hot when no one's home?

MORE TANK TALK In this era of water shortages, it just doesn't make sense to use fresh water to flush our toilets. Wouldn't it be smarter to harness some of the runoff from household sink and shower drains, also called grey water, to be reused for things like flushing? Quebec-based Brac Systems has designed a grey-water recycling system that does exactly that, saving the earth's precious water and your precious cash (www.bracsystems.com).

always hot and ready when you turn on the tap. This means that you are paying and using all that energy to keep the water hot even when no one needs it. A tankless, or on-demand, hot water system activates the heat only when you turn on the tap. The risk is that you may waste water waiting for it to get hot, but the benefit is that you don't waste heating energy. And you'll never run out of hot water again.

#8 Geothermal heat

Get your electricity from above and your heat from below. Geothermal heating takes advantage of stable temperatures below the earth's surface to heat and cool your home. Have you heard of a ground-source heat pump? The idea is that a network of tubes buried two metres underground near your house extracts the heat from below ground, then a pump or compressor circulates that heat through your house. In summer, the system works in reverse, pulling the heat out of your house, the same way a refrigerator works.

You don't have to understand how it works to know that it makes good sense to use free and renewable heat from the earth. The federal government thinks it makes *such* good sense, they offer their highest possible retrofit rebate when you replace your existing heating system with a geothermal heat pump. If you live in Ontario or Saskatchewan, your provincial government will chip in too—you could be looking at a rebate of $7000. A geothermal heating system pays for itself in about four years, and you can say goodbye to your energy bills.

 ## #9 Building materials

Sometimes it's hard being earth-minded about a renovation, since sourcing more sustainable materials can often be more time consuming. Your contractors may roll their eyes when you say you'd like to install counters made of recycled glass bottles or look for non-toxic adhesives, but there is one earth-friendly product they can find easily. Forest Stewardship Council (FSC)–certified lumber— wood that is sustainably harvested from a responsibly managed forest—is carried by more and more building retailers in Canada, including the Home Depot, Rona and other stores (see Chapter 10, "How to Decorate Your House," for more sources of FSC lumber).

For outdoor building projects, be sure to avoid pressure-treated wood—you'll know it by its greenish tint. Although Canada recently banned the use of arsenic in the pressure-treating process, many other hazardous chemicals are still used. Cedar is a naturally weather-resistant wood that is ideal for decks, fences, railings, picnic tables and other exterior projects.

Many composite woods, such as plywood and medium-density fibreboard (MDF), contain formaldehyde, which is used as a binding agent. Even bamboo, the trendy darling of eco-renovation circles, is often treated with formaldehyde for flooring. But formaldehyde is anything but eco-friendly—it's a major respiratory irritant that may cause cancer, *and* it contributes to smog. Be sure to ask for formaldehyde-free wood products. Columbia Forest Products recently converted two factories from using formaldehyde-based binders to soy (www.columbiaforestproducts.com).

#10 Cabinetry and wood panelling

Enough of the invisible stuff; what about renovations that sizzle with style? Even purely aesthetic fixes can be undertaken with an eye on sustainability. Looking at new kitchen cabinets? Remember that most cabinetry is made of some type of particleboard, which is basically compressed sawdust held together with a formaldehyde-based binding agent. You don't want to serve up good home cooking in a kitchen swirling with chemical gasses, do you? Ikea cabinets are formaldehyde free. Or how about storing your whole wheat bread inside your whole wheat cabinets? Wheatboard is made from the wheat stems that are left over after harvesting.

The Canadian manufacturer Viridis makes cabinet boxes and shelves out of similar farming by-products, bound with natural resin binding agents instead of formaldehyde. Their cabinet doors are made of reclaimed or FSC wood, treated with low-VOC or water-based stains and finishes. And Calgary-based Avanti Polymers makes cabinets out of a hemp polymer.

PLASTER DISASTER If you've got a plaster job in your future, be aware that premixed plaster contains preservatives, latex and VOCs. It should be covered quickly with non-VOC primer to seal it and stop further off-gassing. Better still, find a plasterer who will mix traditional plaster, made of gypsum rock and sand, with water for a completely non-off-gassing option.

#11 Countertops and tiles

We expect a lot of our countertops—they need to be able to handle spills, heat and the occasional set of climbing feet. Eco-friendly countertops can do all that and save the earth while they're at it. Paperstone counters are smooth solid surfaces in a range of colours, made with recycled paper. For the sleek modern kitchen there's recycled glass terrazzo counters; for the urban chef look there's a FSC butcher block; and for a versatile, sustainable countertop there's always good old bamboo. Recycled glass tiles create a gorgeous sleek look from nothing but old glass bottles destined for the landfill. They are usually available in a glossy or matte finish.

For more on eco-aesthetics, see Chapter 10, "How to Decorate Your House."

RENO SHOPPING SPREE Where does a green for life Canadian shop for all these healthy home renovation materials? At the Healthiest Home store. Based in Ottawa, they'll ship anywhere in Canada (www.thehealthiesthome.com). GreenWorks Building Supply in Vancouver supplies clean, green building and decorating materials to the West Coast (www.greenworksbuildingsupply.com), and Quebeckers can find a lot of these products at the Coop La Maison Verte in Montreal (www.cooplamaisonverte.com).

Or, you could recycle while you reno. There are 40 Habitat for Humanity ReStores across Canada, stocked with reclaimed building supplies cast off from other projects. Shopping at a ReStore is the green for life trifecta—recycling old stuff, keeping perfectly good materials out of the landfill, and supporting Habitat for Humanity building projects for those in need of housing. Look for a ReStore in your area at www.habitat.org.

[10]
How to Decorate Your House

These days we just can't seem to get enough of home decorating, what with 24-hour TV programming, an entire section at the bookstore and more glossy magazines than you could shake a paint stirstick at. Clearly, ours is a species that wants our nest to look pretty. Yet we're the only animal I know of that is more concerned with making our nest look good than making it healthy for the young we raise there.

But here's what you can't see in all those gorgeous home-decorating magazines: the off-gassing from solvents in the paint, the chemical bath soaking those designer cushions and chairs, the desecration of tropical rainforests to harvest that gorgeous tropical wood, the industrial pollution just to manufacture and transport those tchotchkes from overseas.

THE SCARE:

Polybrominated diphenyl ethers (PBDEs) are used as flame retardants on most mattresses, couches and cushions. They become airborne and migrate from furniture into our lungs and bloodstream. Studies continue to find increasingly high levels of PBDEs accumulated in human blood, fat and breast milk.

Volatile organic compounds (VOCs) are found in most household paints (latex or oil), grouts and glues, pressed wood cabinetry, particleboard and plywood. Exposure to VOCs can cause headaches, nausea, convulsions, respiratory problems and nerve damage and can worsen asthma symptoms.

Formaldehyde, one of the more prevalent VOCs and a known human carcinogen, is used in plywood, glues, particleboard and fibreboard. Home exposure to formaldehyde has been linked to respiratory allergies in children.

According to treehugger.com, 90 percent of the average person's time is spent indoors. Concentrations of VOCs and particulates are 100 times higher indoors than out.

Makes you want to pitch a tent in the park and live there, doesn't it? (Don't do that: tents are made of off-gassing vinyl too.) On the bright side, with a little extra attention to detail, you can make your home earth friendly *and* beautiful. Here are a few things to consider as you fluff your nest.

#1 Furniture

I don't know about your house, but around here, furniture is just a euphemism for play structure. It's occasionally a place to sit, more often a trampoline or secret fort, which is great for the kids' creative development, but it's their physical development that I'm worried about. Those toxic chemicals are released into the air with every bounce and whack of the cushions. If you're buying a new couch or armchair, make low toxicity a priority. Look for products made without PBDEs.

Ikea has eliminated all PBDEs from their cushions, couches, chairs and even mattresses. (PBDEs have not yet been entirely phased out of Ikea's light fixtures.) Otherwise, the sad truth is, most inexpensive furnishings that come and go with trends are likely loaded with PBDEs. Other than more affordable options at Ikea, you'll likely have to buy a higher-end product to avoid them. But here's the bonus: furniture that is well made will be more durable (will withstand more playfights) and last longer, which means it won't wind up in a landfill anytime soon. The most comfortable spot in our house is a loveseat that used to be in my grandmother's house—one non-toxic slipcover to hide the old granny print was all it took to modernize a classic piece. That quality of workmanship has meant four generations have enjoyed it, and who knows how many more to come.

If your grandmother's furniture isn't up for grabs, check out your local Goodwill. Vintage furniture is brilliantly environmental and it meets all three of the Rs—reduce, reuse and recycle. It will cost you a lot less money than buying new, even after you've re-covered it in a gorgeous fabric of your choice. And chances are any off-gassing from the fibres has long since taken place, so it won't pollute the air in your home either—as long as your slipcover is non-toxic too.

Some excellent websites for reusing, or turning one person's trash into your treasure, are eBay and Craigslist. You can unload your old furniture that way too and save it from landfill. Freecycle is a delightful virtual community where you don't have to feel bad about unloading something you don't like onto someone else—it's the home of the pass-along. With almost 300 chapters across Canada, Freecycle provides a community where you can give and get stuff for free. Check it out at www.freecycle.org.

If you're looking to buy any new furniture made of wood—whether tables, chairs, desks, bookshelves or a sofa frame—be sure to look for wood that is Forest Stewardship Council (FSC) certified. The FSC is an organization that certifies forests for sustainable forestry practices. So the trees that were cut down to make your kitchen table were harvested selectively, and proper replanting of the forest was ensured.

Ikea has been a big supporter of FSC products, but check the product before you buy, as not all of their items are made with FSC wood.

If wood furniture suits your style, it doesn't have to be freshly felled. Reclaimed or salvaged wood furniture is made either from trees that were cut in urban centres and would otherwise become firewood (www.urbantreesalvage.com) or from wood previously used in building (www.snoopersfurniture.com; www.lubodesign.com). Available in both modern and classic styles, these wood pieces are so gorgeous and full of character, you'll wonder why you ever bought virgin wood.

One of the most exciting certification standards is called MBDC-C2C. It refers to a cradle-to-cradle approach to manufacturing, born out of the fabulous book by the same name—*Cradle to Cradle: Remaking the Way We Make Things*, by William McDonough and Michael Braungart. It is a must-read for anyone interested in design and an encouraging inspiration for anyone worried about the state of our planet. In a nutshell, C2C certification ensures that everything—from the

DIY WITH FSC **Doing a little DIY? Are you building shelves or a treehouse or anything else with lumber? Ask for wood that is FSC certified, available in Canada at the Home Depot, some Rona stores, GreenWorks Building Supply in Vancouver, Matériaux Coupal in Montreal, West Wind Hardwood on Vancouver Island, and McFadden's in eastern Canada. You'll be ensuring that no old-growth forest is destroyed and that the trees that are harvested are taken selectively and replaced. So, fewer animals have to lose their tree homes so you can build yours.**

materials used to the manufacturing process—is safe and healthy for the environment, but it goes further, ensuring that the end of life for a product is also sustainable. So C2C-certified furniture and other products have been made using the least amount of water, using renewable energy and with parts that are either compostable or entirely recyclable. Now that's what I call green for life. Watch for that standard to blossom and grow.

 ## #2 Bedding

Some of our favourite things happen in our cozy beds, but there's a lot going on in there we'd rather not know about.

We've all heard about dust mites—those multi-legged creepy crawlies that are breeding and eating all around you while you sleep, living off your shed skin cells. But if you thought that was the worst of it, brace yourself. Your mattress was coated with PBDEs—also known as brominated flame retardants (BFRs)—during the manufacturing process, and those toxic chemicals won't just wind up in your nightmares, they'll wind up in your bloodstream.

Canada has officially classified PBDEs as toxic. Although many new mattresses are now made without them, there are lots of PBDE-treated mattresses still sold in stores.

You have a couple of choices for a healthier mattress: Ikea mattresses, like their sofas and chairs, are all PBDE free; organic cotton mattresses are a great option, even though they are less springy than you might like and cost a bit more. Some regular cotton mattresses are treated with borate, a non-toxic flame retardant—a lot of these will be easier to find online. Check out Grassroots (www.grassrootsstore.com), Obasan (www.obasan.ca), the Organic Lifestyle store in Toronto (www.organiclifestyle.ca), or B.C.-based Rawganique (www.rawganique.com), all good Canadian retailers of natural bedding solutions.

They will also be a good source for organic bedsheets. When you consider that we spend roughly a third of our life sleeping and that cotton is the most heavily pesticide-sprayed crop in the world, using a quarter of the world's insecticides, picking the right bedsheets is pretty important for our health. Now, as you might expect, organic cotton sheets are more expensive, but when you do the math they are a good investment. I asked for organic -cotton sheets for Christmas a few years ago and I can't begin to tell you how soft and comfortable they are. No chlorine bleach, no chemical dyes, just cozy cotton so I can sleep easy.

If you are obsessed with wrinkle-free sheets, you may want to remember that formaldehyde is used to make your sheets stay smooth. Still worried about the odd wrinkle? If you really can't stand wrinkled sheets, you can be like my friend Sheila and iron them.

 ## #3 Paint

You know what they say, the cheapest way to decorate is to slap on a new coat of paint. Unfortunately, it's also the best way to fill your house with hazardous chemicals.

Here's what most decor divas leave out: paint is full of benzene, formaldehyde, lead, mercury, methylene chloride, naphthalene and a whole list of other nasty VOCs that will leave you with a bad headache to go with your pretty walls. VOCs contribute to ground-level ozone outdoors and a lot of the air pollution inside your house. U.S. Environmental Protection Agency studies have shown that while that fresh coat of paint is drying on the walls, indoor levels of VOCs are 1000 times higher than outdoor levels.

So what are we going to do about this toxic soup? The first thing you need to do is repeat after me: "I will never use oil-based paint again. Oil-based paints contain 10 to 20 times more VOCs than latex. For whatever painting job I may have, there is a latex product that will work just as well as oil."

Good. Now that we're clear on that, let's get specific about latex paints.

If you want your yellow walls to be truly green, try using a natural paint, made from citrus or other plant ingredients. Natural paints are preservative and pesticide free. (What do you think makes those mildew-resistant paints kill mildew? Biocides, preservatives and fungicides.)

Another good alternative is milk paint, made from milk protein, called casein, with earth pigments added for colour. Milk paint comes in powdered form; just mix with water, and use in a dry area, not a bathroom. Buy only the amount you need, as preservative-free paints store for only a few weeks. All these natural paints are harder to apply, require more coats and take longer to dry, but when you consider that they are solvent, preservative and biocide free, they may just be worth the extra effort.

If you can't find natural paints and you just want a better option at your local paint store, be *sure* to ask for non-VOC latex paint. Low-VOC is available, but non-VOC is even better. It still contains toxic preservatives, but none of the other nasty stuff. My contractor thought I was a nutty fusspot for insisting on non-VOC paint, then was very surprised at what good coverage it had and how pleasantly fume free it was to apply.

If you don't have a large area to cover, look for recycled paint. *Say what?* Just think about it: how many half-empty paint tins are sitting in your basement right now? Donating them to a recycled-paint supplier not only clears space in your basement, it saves the waste of disposing of them and allows someone else to benefit from your fabulous taste in colour. According to the Ecology Action Centre in Nova Scotia, using recycled paint saves roughly a quarter million cans of paint from contaminating the waste stream every year. Boomerang recycled paints are now available in Ontario and Quebec (check out www.boomerangpaint.com).

Careful not to get so excited about applying your new non-toxic natural paint that you go slapping on hazardous chemicals to remove the old stuff. Most paint strippers contain methylene chloride, a probable human carcinogen. Some are made with caustic soda, which can cause burns and lung irritation. The best way to remove old paint is with mineral washing soda (sodium carbonate), available in the laundry section of your supermarket. Wearing gloves, mix the washing soda with water until it forms a thick paste. Using a putty knife, spread it on the surface to be stripped and leave it overnight, misting with water whenever possible. Rinse and peel off the paint.

THE HUMANE STAIN The same nasty VOC story is true of stains and varnishes too. Unfortunately, low-VOC and non-formaldehyde sealants and stains, made from natural pigments, are often difficult to find in Canada. You can order online from companies in the United States like Weather-Bos (www.weatherbos.com) and Livos (www.livos.us). In Canada, look for the AFM line of wood finishes and sealants at www.thehealthiesthome.com. See Chapter 3, "How to Clean the Kitchen," for recipes and suggestions for keeping wood floors naturally clean.

Before you remove any old paint, be sure to check for lead content—ask at your paint store for a lead-testing kit. If you're not sure how old the paint job is, best to leave it be. Paint over it—*don't* sand it or strip it.

If you ever need to strip old non-lead paint or otherwise prepare a surface for painting, look for Removall products, made by Napier Technologies in B.C. They offer a complete line of water-based, non-toxic and biodegradable products for interior and exterior jobs. Check out www.biowash.com for more information.

For more detail on sourcing non-toxic paints, removers and sealants, check out the Healthiest Home store or website (www.thehealthiesthome.com).

There's a greener way to clean up after your paint job too. First of all, for an ongoing project, you don't need to clean your brushes every day. Wrap brushes or rollers in a plastic bag, squeeze out any air pockets and store in a dark place. Kept this way, brushes will last up to a week and be soft and ready to continue painting as soon as they are unwrapped. (This works for brushes used on paint but not varnish.)

When you do finally finish the job you can wash your brushes and hands (and in my case, hair, occasionally feet) in soap and water. But don't wash them in the sink! Although latex paint is less detrimental than oil-based paint, it is still full of solvents, pigments and additives that contaminate the groundwater and damage fish and wildlife. Wash your brushes in a bucket with water. Pour the dirty water into a sealable container, and take it to a hazardous waste depot with your paint cans.

#4 Flooring

When I grew up, anyone with a bit of decorating know-how had shag carpeting on all their floors. Now we know that dust and airborne pollutants get trapped in rug fibres, and that those fibres themselves are often made of synthetic polymers that will off-gas into the rest of the house. So what's the informed decorator to do? There are lots of good options for sustainable flooring.

Carpet makes for the coziest floor covering, but you should be aware of its downsides as well. According to Consumer Reports, the two best-selling carpet fibres are nylon and olefin, both synthetics. They are both derived from petroleum, which as we know wreaks havoc on the earth. Plus, synthetic carpets off-gas a wacky stew of harmful gases.

As most people with allergies have learned, carpets trap dust and other particulates, including a shocking amount of airborne toxins: pesticides from neighbouring lawns, mercury and lead from the street. Add to that the dander from pets and bacteria trampled in on street shoes, and your carpet is jam-packed with yucky stuff. And that's just the side you can see. Carpets are usually backed with nylon (petroleum-derived) webbing. Underneath *that*, what's making it soft underfoot? Synthetic padding, attached to your floor using chemical adhesives that release fumes into your home long after they've been applied. Pretty crazy to think about, especially if you've got little children crawling and drooling and exploring all over those floors.

If you have to get carpet, choose 100 percent wool with jute backing, or any backing that is sewn on rather than glued. Use carpet tacks rather than adhesives to secure your carpeting. The carpets we have in certain parts of our house are pure wool, and while they were more expensive than synthetic, they have never given me a headache the way some off-gassing carpets do. The only headaches I get are from my boys running on the freshly cleaned carpet without taking off their dirty running shoes.

Now before you go putting down hardwood floors in place of all your toxic carpets, bear in mind that hardwood comes with its own set of complications. New hardwood means you're contributing to deforestation, of course, but if you buy salvaged wood flooring (www.canadianheritagetimber.com) or FSC-certified products (see #1, above), you're way ahead. Salvaged wood gets a second life in your home—and that reclaimed wood makes for a highly coveted designer look. Your best bet, which is widely available, is glueless floating flooring, attached with nails rather than glues. Be sure to treat and stain any wood flooring with low-VOC finishes.

Bamboo floors are an increasingly popular alternative to hardwood and are even more durable. Bamboo plants are hearty and fast growing, so they need virtually no pesticides to grow, and they replace themselves in a matter of a few years. So from a sustainability perspective, they're a home run. But don't cancel out the environmental gain of using a renewable fibre by installing it with toxic glue or treating it with VOC-emitting sealants. As always, make sure your stain, sealant or polish is low VOC.

Cork is another tree that regrows quickly, so it too makes for a greener alternative to hardwood. Cork floors are installed in a free-floating fashion, sitting on the subfloor while not actually attached to it. This means that no glues are used, and also that they are well suited to older

BE CHOOSY ABOUT YOUR BAMBOO Because of the way they are cured, most hardwoods, including bamboo, can off-gas formaldehyde—ask for formaldehyde-free bamboo flooring. Check out www.bamboomountain.com, www.greenfloors.com or www.bamboohardwoods.com.

homes where nothing is even after the foundations have settled.

In a more modern design, poured concrete is a very green flooring solution. Unheated concrete may sound like a chilly option underfoot for a cold Canadian morning, but it actually keeps a constant temperature year-round, which improves the energy efficiency of your home. As long as it is treated with low-VOC sealants and polishes, it is water resistant, and it won't collect allergens or dust mites. The materials used to create concrete are sustainable. If you add to the mix recycled crushed concrete or fly ash—a waste product from coal combustion plants—it becomes an even more elegant solution.

Stone floors offer the same allergen- and dust-free surface, but be sure that the stone is native to your area— ideally from a smaller-scale quarry that has less of an impact on the surrounding environment. Imported tile flooring has a bigger carbon footprint, travelling halfway around the world. Look for locally produced tiles or some of the many options made with postconsumer waste materials, including recycled industrial glass.

Most of us have had vinyl flooring in our homes at some point in our lives. Whether in sheets or tiles, polyvinyl chloride (PVC) is the most popular choice for inexpensive, durable flooring. It's also one of the most hazardous. As its name suggests, PVC contains both chlorine and plasticizers, specifically phthalates, including DEHP. According to a report from National Geographic's online magazine *The Green Guide*, plasticizers like DEHP make up roughly 27 percent of vinyl sheet flooring by weight. DEHP is a probable human carcinogen, known to cause chronic health problems; because phthalates like DEHP do not bond to the plastic, they can migrate from the product. Ironically, most people put in vinyl floors to deal with messy kids, but given how much time they spend crawling and playing on them, it's the vinyl floors that are messing up the kids.

Before vinyl became the chemical solution to affordable flooring, linoleum was the floor covering of choice. And, as Grandma knows best, it turns out linoleum is actually a wise choice for sustainability. Made primarily from linseed oil, pine resin, sawdust and cork dust, linoleum is practically biodegradable. As long as you have it installed without glues—as with all laminate options, remember the glueless floating floor—linoleum makes an excellent green floor.

We covered the floor of our back hall, the most heavily trafficked area in our house, with marmoleum, a non-toxic floor covering made from wood pulp. It comes in a rainbow of fun colours, wipes up in a snap, and has withstood several years of three stomping boys. It is installed with non-toxic glue—check out www.themarmoleumstore.com for more information.

 ## Shower curtains

In the otherwise fairly monochromatic palette of the bathroom, the shower curtain can be a bit of a character statement. The world map, the *New York Times* motif, tropical fish, jazzy stripes—they add a funky punch. But the problem is that most of those cool designs are printed onto PVC curtains, and the punch they deal out is anything but funky. Your PVC shower curtain is downright soaked in petrochemicals.

Think of how it smells when you open it up and first use it—that potent plastic odour is the off-gassing from the polyvinyl chloride, and it's likely carcinogenic and hormone disrupting.

Look for curtains that are made of non-chlorinated vinyl, which will be labelled EVA or PEVA. Ikea comes through again on this one: none of their shower curtains are made with PVC. You can also go for an organic cotton curtain, or even hemp. Check out Grassroots (www.grassrootsstore.com) or Organic Lifestyle (www.organiclifestyle.ca) for those.

#6 Towels

Don't be a slave to the whims of the design magazines. Unless you actually need to buy new towels right now, the most green for life thing you can do is keep using the ones you have, and treat them with care. I'm still using a few of the towels from my childhood, castoffs from my parents. As my mother always says, good quality is worth the investment. But when it comes time for new towels, avoid the environmental assault on wildlife, water systems and ultimately your skin from insecticide-soaked cotton— look for ones made of organic cotton or hemp, which are becoming widely available. Those Egyptian cotton towels

---

WHAT'S THE SWEDISH FOR CORPORATE LEADER?
For all the driving they demand with their big box locations, the transportation emissions racked up by their offshore manufacturing and shipping, and the trees chopped down to make their catalogues (and all the anxiety and marriage counselling brought on by those darn assemble-it-yourself bookcases), Ikea stores have put their best corporate responsibility foot forward where other mainstream multinational companies have lagged. They phased phthalates out of their plastics and toys over a decade ago; they're partnered with the World Wildlife Fund to support FSC wood certification and programs that produce more environmentally friendly cotton; and they sell no furniture or mattresses treated with the toxic fire retardants PBDEs. Let's give credit where credit is due and wave a little Swedish flag in appreciation.

(or sheets) sound exotic and luxurious, but they likely involve unsavoury violations of child labour laws in Egypt. In its 2001 report on child labour in Egypt's cotton fields, Human Rights Watch cites the one million children between age 7 and 12 working 11-hour days for Egypt's agricultural co-operatives to manually remove pests from cotton plants. That's just no way to spend a childhood.

You can find bamboo everywhere now, from T-shirts to flooring—why not on the towel rack? Bamboo towels are available through the Organic Lifestyle store and website (www.organiclifestyle.com), and you can get hemp towels through www.rawganique.com. Lyocell is a relatively new and sustainable fibre to look out for, made from wood cellulose, usually sourced from sustainably managed forests. Lyocell towels are soft, durable and ultimately biodegradable. Another good reason to pick your wet towel up off the floor and hang it to dry.

[11]
How to **Buy a Car**

A friend with two children once cautioned me about my urge to have a third child. She made the case that when you jump from being a family of four to anything bigger, it's an exponential increase in complication, as well as chaos. Travel packages are usually based on a family of four, she pointed out, and restaurant tables seat four comfortably, to say nothing of cars. And it's true. Our choice of car—especially a green one—is dramatically influenced by having more than two kids.

Well, we know how this story goes, don't we? My friend drives her two children around comfortably in a Toyota Prius, one of the most fuel-efficient cars ever made. My husband and I, while we have no regrets about bringing our third wonderful son into the world, scrape our knuckles and pull out our hair trying to buckle all three of our kids into an even slightly earth-friendly car.

As the dire effects of global warming became harder and harder to ignore, we made a commitment in our family not to buy a car that wasn't the best possible choice for the environment. But as we are not the first to find out, that is easier said than done! When the lease on our last car expired, we still hadn't found a car we could all squeeze into that wouldn't guzzle undue amounts of gas. So for several months, we biked, hiked and borrowed wheels until we finally came up with a solution. Here's what we asked ourselves along the way.

#1 Do you really need to buy one?

You never know how easily you can survive without a car until you have to. You'll soon find that you can get to meetings on time and keep the fridge full of food, and you won't be paying those monthly car insurance and leasing costs.

For the days that you do need a car, there's always car sharing. The simple idea of using a car when you need it and leaving it for someone else when you're done was first launched in Switzerland in 1987 and came to Canada a few years later. As of January 2007, nearly 22,000 Canadians had joined car-sharing programs, according to Car Sharing Canada.

The idea is simple. You book a car for when and where you need it, then pick it up and drop it off at any number of convenient locations in your community. Check out www.carsharing.ca for the organization nearest you.

I have a friend with four kids who doesn't own a car and swears by it. She rents when she needs one—and these days you can even rent a hybrid (see #3, below, for why you want a hybrid). More and more car rental companies are adding hybrids to their fleets, including Discount in Ontario and ViaRoute in Quebec. Hertz has recently added a few thousand hybrids to 50 airport locations across the United States. Ask for a hybrid at Enterprise rentals—they are introducing them into more markets every month.

Another adventurous way to get from A to B without wheels of your very own is to carpool. Check out www.vivacommute.com to find rideshare services for your commute or find fellow carpoolers in your area. Or if you're a car owner looking for company on your commute, you can start your own car pool through the website too.

 ## #2 What kind of car do you need?

The first principle of green for life shopping is to buy based on need, not just on want. So, ask yourself, do you really *need* an SUV?

Sport utility vehicles use 30 percent more gas than other cars, and because they're classified as light trucks, they aren't manufactured to meet strict emissions standards. If that's not enough to turn you off SUVs, they're also less safe than regular cars, according to Malcolm Gladwell's 2004 *New Yorker* article "Big and Bad" (read the article at www.gladwell.com). Schlepping the kids to the mall hardly counts as off-road driving, so leave the light trucks to the mountain rangers.

Studies show that a typical car produces roughly three times its weight in carbon dioxide emissions every year, so a good general rule is the lighter your car, the better its fuel efficiency. The extra weight of four-wheel drive or all-wheel drive can increase your fuel consumption by 10 percent compared with two-wheel drive. And those bells and whistles like power windows, seats and mirrors? They make our lives more convenient, but remember, they'll cost you more and increase your gas costs because of all the extra weight.

Like household appliances, cars are rated for efficiency, so look for the EnerGuide label found on all new passenger cars and passenger trucks. The label will tell you the city and highway fuel consumption of the vehicle and give you an estimate for annual fuel costs. The EU recently voted that car advertising in Europe must include warnings about carbon dioxide emissions and fuel consumption. Maybe someday that onus will be on manufacturers here in North America as well.

Until then, the single best tool for making car purchase decisions is the Natural Resources Canada (NRCan) fuel-efficient vehicle list. It lets you compare new vehicles based on mileage and fuel costs, and it's updated every year as new models arrive. You can also see past lists to compare fuel efficiency if you're buying a used car. Check out the personal transportation link at www.oee.nrcan.gc.ca.

#3 Should it be a hybrid?

In a car market where fuel economy has actually gotten worse since the 1908 Ford Model T (25 miles per gallon then, 16 MPG average now), the 40 percent mileage improvement from a hybrid engine is downright exciting. Have you ever taken a spin in one of these part gas engine/part battery-operated cars? They drive exactly like a regular car until, all of a sudden—silence. The engine shuts off, but the car keeps moving! The battery half of the hybrid engine is charged by the friction when you apply the brakes. And so whenever it can, the car stops using the combustion engine and runs on the battery alone.

Now, as more and more car manufacturers get on the hybrid bandwagon, you should know that not all hybrids are created equal. In broad strokes, Toyota has been making hybrid engines for the longest time and has the most models available. In fact, several other car companies simply license the technology from Toyota for their own hybrid vehicles. Saturn offers the most affordable hybrids, though their efficiency is not as impressive. Ford

SHIFT TO SAVINGS Do you drive stick? If not, now's the time to learn. Manual transmission is more fuel efficient than automatic. If you do have to buy automatic, look for a vehicle with more gears, if possible.

has promised to hybridize half of its fleet by 2010; the Escape Hybrid uses the Toyota technology. Nissan and Honda have fewer entries in the hybrid game, but their models rate very high for fuel efficiency.

THE BATTLE OF THE HYBRIDS Here are NRCan's fuel-efficiency ratings for hybrids, from highest to lowest:

> Toyota Prius
> Honda Civic Hybrid
> Toyota Camry Hybrid
> Nissan Altima Hybrid
> Ford Escape Hybrid
> Saturn Aura
> Saturn Vue
> Toyota Highlander

Fuel consumption differs significantly among these models; to compare, check out www.oee.nrcan.gc.ca/transportation/tools/fuelratings.

THE FUTURE OF THE HYBRID What's better than a gas-electric hybrid car? A gas-electric hybrid with a souped-up battery that goes twice as far on electricity alone. Hymotion is a new product that is installed in your hybrid vehicle and converts it to a plug-in hybrid. Charging your battery overnight—during off-peak hours when electricity production is at its greenest—doubles your hybrid's fuel economy. You could do all your city driving gas free. For 2008, Hymotion adapters are available only for the Toyota Prius, though they are planning to expand their range. The founders of Google have so much faith in this kind of plug-in hybrid electric vehicle (PHEV), or "plug-in," that they have just put up $10 million U.S. for the development of more. All the more reason to buy a hybrid, so you can eventually convert it to a plug-in. Check out www.hymotion.com.

Driving these cool cars comes with even more perks. For example, Ikea offers hybrid drivers the best parking spots, you can use commuter lanes, and you can get rebates of up to $5000 from the federal and some provincial governments.

#4 What about biodiesel?

At Discovery Channel in the late 1990s, I interviewed a groovy couple from California who were making science news by running their vehicle (a VW Westfalia, natch) on old french fry oil. They had converted their diesel engine to run on nothing but vegetable oil. Not only were the emissions less hazardous to the environment than regular diesel, but the fumes from the tailpipe of their vehicle smelled like delicious golden fries. Fast forward a decade, and while we're hardly smelling french fry exhaust at every stoplight, biodiesel has certainly come into its own. They're set to break ground just north of Calgary for a brand new biodiesel plant, the ninety-fourth such facility in North America.

You don't need to adapt a diesel engine to run on biofuel—when Dr. Rudolf Diesel developed the engine in the late nineteenth century, it was designed to run on peanut oil. These days, commercial biodiesel, available at

BUY YOUR VEGETABLE OIL IN BULK **Now if there is a diesel vehicle in your driveway but no biodiesel pump nearby, what about running it on straight vegetable oil (SVO)? You don't have to pull up to the back of a diner to get used vegetable oil—although that is probably the cheapest source possible. Professional outfits like PlantDrive in B.C. (www.plantdrive.ca) or ecoauto in Montreal (www.ecoauto.ca) can adapt your regular diesel engine to run on SVO—start filling your shopping cart with mega jugs and drive home carbon neutral.**

select gas stations, is anywhere from 5 to 20 percent bio—usually derived from soy, canola or palm—and the rest is regular diesel.

I live near one of the three gas stations in all of Toronto that currently offer biodiesel at the pumps, but those stations are rare: there is only a handful in all of Canada right now. Even if you can access biodiesel at the pumps, it is not without its drawbacks. Friends who drive cars that run on commercial biodiesel say their cars can be a little sluggish in cold weather, depending on the percentage of bio in the blend. Worse than that, though, is the ironic environmental spinoff issue: when you add up all the agricultural land required for biofuel crops, all the pesticides sprayed on the plants, and the carbon footprint of processing and transportation, it doesn't seem quite as green an alternative anymore.

Now, if you're going around to restaurants and taking the old grease out of their fryers, saving it from disposal to use in your engine, you are definitely hardcore green. To you, I tip my vintage hemp hat. For the rest of us looking to drive cleaner without having to get our hands too dirty, biodiesel may not be the greenest choice.

I checked out www.grist.org (a green for life favourite site) to help me make this decision, and they definitely favoured hybrid over biodiesel.

#5 What to do with your old one?

If you're investing in a new car to lighten your load on the earth, it hardly makes sense to send your old jalopy around the block with someone else behind the wheel. That $800 you get for selling it doesn't justify all the pollution it's still cranking out—the average 12-year-old vehicle produces roughly 17 times more smog-forming emissions than a new one. So don't give your old car to your kid brother, give him a bus pass. And send ole' Bessie to Car Heaven, a national program run by the Clean Air Foundation. They'll tow your car away for free, recycle it in an environmentally responsible manner, and leave you with any number of goodies. Depending on where you live, it could be a $1000 coupon toward the purchase of a new GM car, a tax receipt from the charity of your choice, or $300 toward the purchase of a new bike. Check out www.carheaven.ca for more information.

#6 Still waiting for the technology to catch up?

"The Toyota Sienna minivan will be out in hybrid by 2009...." "The Volvo wagon will be available in diesel in North America sometime in the next two years...." If I had a dime for every green vehicle that wasn't quite ready for commercial release, I'd buy you a fair trade coffee.

The demand for greener cars is growing—that much we know. A 2006 Environics poll showed that Canadian drivers' awareness of fuel efficiency is twice as high as it's ever been. I think most of us have noticed how much more it hurts to pay for a fill-up at the pump. Industry will catch up to public demand eventually, but until it does, you don't want to hand over money for a new car you don't really want.

Leasebusters lets you take over someone else's lease for the remainder of their term—sometimes for just a few months. So you can lease a more fuel-efficient car until the one you really want is out on the market. Check out www.leasebusters.ca—just be very clear on why the previous leasee is giving up the car (from personal experience, let me recommend having it inspected for evidence of any accident history).

Now you know everything I wish I had known when it came time to replace our car. So I bet you're just dying to know, after all that, what became the wheels of choice for my family of five.

While we still walk to school and bike to get groceries, we now do our necessary driving in a Ford Escape Hybrid. When we scrolled down NRCan's list of new cars, in descending order of fuel efficiency, the Escape was the first one we could fit our family into. (And only barely, I might add. Let's hope buying a green for life car is a heck of a lot easier by the time they're teenagers.)

Since the Escape is next on the list for conversion to a battery range extender like the Hymotion plug-in adapter, our gas-electric hybrid will soon be even more electric.

Then, just so no one out there mistakes us for a gas-guzzling SUV, we'll emblazon the side of our car with decals that boast of our fuel-efficient choices and that promote greener driving options. I know, I have no shame—just a burning desire to see people empowered to make better choices for the earth. It shouldn't have to be this hard.

[12]
How to **Drive a Car**

It was my eldest son's first word: car (except it sounded more like cah-cah). Who could blame the little urban baby for having a significant linguistic breakthrough over the ubiquitous automobile? We may recycle, we may pop in a compact fluorescent bulb here and there, we may even buy the occasional organic apple. But we just can't seem to shake our addiction to the convenience of the cah-cah.

Those handy little inventions do get us where we want to go without the need for horse and buggy, but they're also getting us into a lot of trouble, environmentally speaking.

According to Statistics Canada's 2006 Households and the Environment survey, a quarter of Canada's greenhouse gas emissions come from transportation, and half of that amount comes from personal passenger use—regular folks like us scrambling to make it to the movie on time or taking the kids to hockey practice.

Now, as much as we might like to give up those 6 a.m. hockey practices, the reality is that the 83 percent of Canadians who own cars are going to continue to use them. The goal is to figure out how to use your car and still be green for life. So, let's see what we can do.

Leave it in park

While you should certainly read on for lots of ways to make your driving habits more green for life, I still think it's a good idea to ask yourself every single day, do I *really* need to take the car to get there?

I know. Your car is warm when it's cold outside, and cool when it's hot outside. It's private and it's got a little spot for your coffee and you can play your favourite music. But when pregnant women are being told to stay indoors on a fairly regular basis each summer in major cities because of smog advisories, and when nationwide smog-related deaths now exceed fatalities from breast cancer, prostate cancer and motor vehicle accidents combined, we have to weigh that personal comfort and convenience against the bigger picture and rethink our dependence on our wheels.

David Suzuki talked to me once in an interview about our disconnect as human beings, and how we fail to see the link between our habits and their effects. He says he once watched in the busy emergency room of a Toronto hospital on a smog alert day as people burst in with their loved ones who were having trouble breathing due to asthma and respiratory troubles. When he asked the worried and upset families how they got their sick loved ones to the hospital that day, they looked at him blankly and said, "In our SUV, of course. Why?"

Think about how much you drive. Think about whether there are any ways you could change that. Look for opportunities in your week to walk, ride your bike, take public transit or carpool instead. You'll be amazed at how much better you'll feel. Walking and biking reconnect you with the world around you and make you healthier too.

#2 Think before you drive

I'm sure you don't need me to tell you how expensive it is to fuel, park and maintain your car every year. One thing you can do to reduce your amount of driving is called trip chaining. Sounds like some whacked-out holdover from the 1960s involving narcotics, but it's actually just about planning your errands. Do you ever feel like you're getting in and out of your car a thousand times in a single day? Try to plan your route so you can streamline your travel—take back the library books on the same day you do your grocery shopping. Choose a grocery store near the gym or the office. You get the idea. Trip chaining is a more efficient use of your gas *and* your time.

#3 Drive the speed limit

If you have to drive, try driving the speed limit. As a recovering leadfoot, I understand how hard it can be to stay within the limits of the law. But not only is it safer and less stressful, driving the speed limit makes sense. Engines are designed to operate most efficiently at the speed limit, so when you cruise the highway at 120 km/hour instead of the recommended limit of 100 km/hour, you are increasing your fuel consumption by 20 percent. And have you

> PLAN YOUR DAY Natural Resources Canada says that any trip that's less than five kilometres doesn't allow the car's engine to reach its most efficient operating temperature, which means you'll use more gas and create more emissions on a short trip. Run those errands on a day when you have more to do—you'll use less gas if you do them when your car is already warmed up.

noticed how the guy whizzing past you in city traffic just to make the light is still right beside you at the next light three blocks away? According to Natural Resources Canada, European tests have shown that aggressive "jackrabbit" driving reduced travel time by a grand total of 4 percent but increased fuel consumption by 37 percent, and increased some toxic emissions by 500 percent. So slow down, keep a steady speed and enjoy the ride.

#4 Don't idle your car

This is a pet peeve of mine. You may be reading this book and looking at my picture and saying to yourself, "Oh yeah, I recognize her! She's the lady who stuck her head in my window and asked me to turn off my engine!" Yes, that was me. Oh, I try to be nice about it, I really do. I usually just smile and make a wrist-flicking gesture—isn't that the universal symbol for "Please turn off your ignition"? My husband tries throwing in mention of global warming (idling is his pet peeve too), and that often seems to help.

THE IDLE-FREE ZONE If idling cars are your pet peeve too, arm yourself with more information. Check out the Idle-Free Zone at www.oee.nrcan.gc.ca/communities-government/. You can find more information on idling, flyers to hand out to idlers to inform them of why they should stop, and even a script of what to say when you approach people running their car engines. And you can learn how to start a no-idling campaign at your school. The only thing worse than spewing noxious emissions from idling cars is spewing them in front of the school-yard, where kids need clean air during their active outdoor play.

Because it's true. If you didn't know this before, let me make it clear: leaving your engine running for more than 10 seconds—that's right *10 seconds*—is a waste of gas and creates unnecessary greenhouse gas emissions.

When you idle your car, the engine is running below peak temperature. Without getting into too much detail, let's just say that not running at peak temperature means that some gunky stuff builds up on some important parts that are supposed to be able to move easily and be gunk free, so it's actually bad for your car—not just the air—to idle your car.

Some people think it's better for your car to leave the engine running. That's like thinking that it uses more electricity to turn the lights back on after you turn them off. Wrong. And wrong again. If you're idling your car for more than 10 seconds, it's using more gas than it would take to restart your engine.

#5 Check your tire pressure

No matter what brand of tires you buy, they're only as safe as the care you put into keeping them properly inflated. Studies show that more than half of Canadian drivers don't know how or when to check tire pressure. In fact, 70 percent of cars on the road in this country have underinflated tires. Tires that are underinflated create greater drag on the road and less efficient (and less safe) handling of your vehicle.

The right way to check tire pressure is to do it when the tires are cold, which means when the car has been driven two kilometres or less in the last three hours. You'll find a sticker with your car's pressure recommendations inside the doorframe of the driver's door. Check your tire pressure once a month, more often in winter, especially after a sharp drop in temperature. You will be doing the earth a favour and saving money at the same time. Remember, driving with poorly inflated tires uses more gas.

#6 Change your oil change habits

The healthier your car is, the better it will run, and the easier it will be on the earth—it's as simple as that. Regular tune-ups may cost you a few dollars, but they easily pay for themselves in overall fuel savings. When your car is in top condition, it uses fuel and oil most efficiently.

The general recommendation for oil changes is every three months or five thousand kilometres, whichever comes first. If you do it yourself, be sure to dispose of the oil properly. Put it in a clean, sealable container and take it to your local hazardous waste facility.

If you prefer to let others get their hands dirty, ask your mechanic to see that your old oil gets recycled, and request recycled oil for your replacement. Or bring your own—Autoprix from Zellers is a re-refined motor oil that is both green and affordable. Some transmission oils in

MAKE A BETTER CHOICE AT THE PUMP When you pull up to the pump, be judicious about which gas provider you support. Many of the most significant environmental non-government organizations (ENGOs) in Canada, including the David Suzuki Foundation, Greenpeace and the Sierra Club, all advise us not to fill up at Esso. Of all the petroleum companies, they say Esso has the worst environmental track record, and shows the least interest in improving it. Check out www.stopesso.ca for more information. In the meantime, fill up at Sunoco stations whenever possible. Since 1993, Sunoco has integrated many principles from the CERES code of environmental business practices. As multinational giants of pollution and exploitation go, Sunoco's the best of the bunch.

industrial use are derived from plant material—ask your mechanic if any bio-based oils are available for your car.

#7 Improve your winter driving

While the global warming effect of all our driving may be that we have warmer winters, there are still lots of chilly Canadian mornings when taking the car is the most comfortable choice. But since cars actually use more fuel in the cold weather just to function smoothly, it's important to know how to mitigate the extra cost and environmental assault of winter driving.

The combustion of the fuel is less efficient in cold weather. Like you, going out the door with a shiver on a cold morning, your car needs some time to get the joints running smoothly. *But don't idle your car to warm it up!* Natural Resources Canada says the best way to warm up your car is to drive it. A block heater is an excellent investment to help warm up a cold engine in the morning. If you set a timer on the block heater for two hours before you plan to drive away, it will take the chill out of the lubricants and the stress out of a cold morning start.

Be sure to clear *all* the snow off your car, especially the hard-to-reach bits where the windshield meets the car hood. The air intake for the defroster is there, and if it's got snow on it, it will draw moisture into the venting system and make even more fog on the windshield.

[13]
How to **Wash a Car**

There are many times when the path to eco-lightenment is also the path of least effort, and washing your car is one of them. When it comes to keeping your car clean, you definitely want to label yourself an environmentalist. Every good green for lifer knows that the most eco-friendly way to wash your car is not to wash it yourself. Let the professionals handle that one for you.

#1 Take it to the cleaners

In the same way that an automatic dishwasher will always beat handwashing dishes for efficiency of water, energy and soap (see Chapter 2, "How to Wash the Dishes"), those professional car wash operations will always be greener than you and your five-year-old on the front lawn with the green garden hose.

Here's why: all the junk that you want to get off your car to make it shine and sparkle is the very same stuff that takes the shine and sparkle out of natural water systems and the wildlife that lives there.

The runoff from car washing contains detergents, surfactants and degreasers from the soap, plus all the oils, rust, engine grime, wax and other street dust that's built up on your car. When you do the job yourself, as industrious as you might feel, you're sending that industrial storm of pollution right down the sewer and into the nearest water system, untreated.

Professional car washes—usually out of financial self-interest, not environmental high-mindedness, but who cares—are much more judicious in their use of water. The average home wash uses as much as 440 litres. A commercial car wash uses less than half that amount. Plus, those facilities are usually built with a filtering system in the collection tank so that the contaminants are removed before the water is routed on to a sewage treatment facility.

Check out www.riversides.org/riversafe for more information on a Canadian campaign to educate car owners about the environmental impact of car washing.

#2 Make your fundraiser pollution free

If your kids, or people in your community, are planning a car-washing event to raise money, check in with the RiverSafe Carwash Campaign (see above) before you start spraying the suds. They will provide you free of charge with a collection mat to absorb some of the runoff, environmentally friendly soaps and everything else you will need to make your fundraising event fun and safe, for you and for the earth.

#3 DIY the right way

If you really have to wash your car yourself, or if you have no access to a commercial car wash, at least do it responsibly. Think about what else might result from your actions, other than a shiny vehicle. Wash the car using biodegradable cleaning products—or better yet, use only water, no soaps (it's the drying that makes it shine, not the soap). Wash it on the lawn, not on the road, so the runoff is filtered through the ground and won't run directly through the storm sewer into rivers, lakes and streams. Use a hose with a spray nozzle, preferably with an on/off switch so you don't waste water.

[14]
How to **Go Shopping**

The town where my grandfather grew up is a beautiful historic centre in the Ottawa Valley, a pretty, bustling riverside community. Or at least it was, before the big box stores set up shop on the outskirts of town. Now, like so many cities and towns across North America, it has a less active main street, fewer pedestrians, more car traffic, and sprawling parking lots and malls eating up what used to be wilderness.

Of course, we can't blame anybody but ourselves for these big box monstrosities: I have yet to see one go out of business. If they build them, we will come, apparently.

Because heaven knows, we do love to consume. A new car rolls off the line every second. More than 2 million shoes are bought and sold every single day. It's nothing short of terrifying to think of all the stuff that is manufactured, shipped, bought, sold, junked and dumped worldwide, often in short order. Looking at North America from space, the highest point on the eastern seaboard is a landfill.

Yes, what you buy and where you buy it has a ripple effect, long after the excitement of the purchase wears off. So here's how to make your retail therapy a little more therapeutic for the earth.

#1 Shop less

Maybe we all have enough. The central tenet of environmentalism really is about consuming less. Less energy, less stuff. It's not all that sexy or fun, but it's the hard truth. It sounds downright heretical, doesn't it? In the credit card age, the global economy, we buy pretty much whatever we want, *because we can*.

In 2003, *New Scientist* magazine reported that the more consumer goods you have, the more you think you need to make yourself happy. Force yourself to think about the energy and materials it took to make and transport whatever you have the urge to buy. And ask yourself where it will go when you're done with it—we throw out more than 12 million tons of household solid waste every year in this country.

#2 Shop in your community

Whenever you can—I realize that depending on where you live, this may not always be possible—buy from the vendors in your neighbourhood. When I interviewed Robert F. Kennedy Jr. for the Discovery Channel, he said

FIND OUT MORE ABOUT SHOPPING LESS In 1992, *Adbusters* created Buy Nothing Day on the last Friday of November—traditionally the biggest shopping day of the year in the United States. Since then, activists worldwide have joined the celebrations to draw attention to our shopping addiction. To find out more, check out www.adbusters.org. Too serious for you? Try a lighter take: "What Would Jesus Buy?" is a fun and provocative documentary about the Church of Stop Shopping. Check out www.revbilly.com. Or read *Cradle to Cradle* by William McDonough and Michael Braungart. Their vision of sustainable manufacturing makes you look at your purchases in a new light.

if he could wave a magic wand to make environmental change, the first thing he would do is get rid of malls. Malls mean natural spaces are cleared and covered with cement. Supporting local business is good for both social and environmental health. Local business people have a stake in the community—they are more likely to treat it with care and environmental stewardship. Successful local shops foster relationships, with individuals and with schools and community teams. And if the old-fashioned, small-town feeling of knowing your shopkeepers doesn't do it for you, maybe the increase in housing prices from a vibrant local business community will.

 ## Shop locally made

So much of what we wear, play with and otherwise use is made in China or some other faraway place. Most purchases in Canada support another economy's manufacturing sector, are made using materials regulated by laws and standards that Canadians are largely unfamiliar with (and might not agree with if they were) and contribute significantly to greenhouse gases by being shipped halfway around the world to get to our store shelves.

The only thing you can do is check the label. Where there is a choice, opt for the item made closer to home. Search the Internet for Canadian manufacturers of whatever you need to buy (see #5, below, for more on green shopping online). We are swimming upstream on this one, but wherever possible, shop local. You know how true it is for food and produce, now imagine putting your family on the 100 mile diet for products and services too.

 ## BYO bags

Did you know that in some parts of the world, if you don't bring your own bag to the store you'll be carrying your purchases home in your pockets? That's right, as foreign a concept as it may be to us in North America, there are places where the use of petroleum by-products for the mass production of plastic bags that get used once then thrown away is seen as wasteful, and it just doesn't happen.

Canadians, on the other hand, take home more than 55 million shopping bags each week. Many of these bags wind up ingested by waterfowl, in landfill where they take lifetimes to break down, or hanging in tree branches.

Designer Anya Hindmarch took action against the problem and created an unprecedented shopping frenzy with her affordable line of reusable shopping bags that have "I'm Not a Plastic Bag" written on the side. They quickly sold out, but there are plenty of other stylish sustainable bags to carry your stuff home in. The key is to have them with you at the checkout, and not hanging on a hook in your front hall. Choose a lightweight, collapsible option that folds up into nothing and stays in your purse. My Envirosax bag is a regular subject of conversation at the checkout counter for how tiny it is in my purse and how huge an amount of stuff it can carry when I open it up (www.envirosax.com). The EZ bag is available through www.reallynatural.com. Check out more jazzy choices from www.reusablebags.com and the Canadian eco-chic bagmaker www.posch.ca.

 ## #5 Shop online

If you cannot buy from vendors up the road or around the corner, there is an environmental case to be made for letting your mouse do your shopping. E-commerce warehouses use one-sixteenth the amount of energy to operate than the average retail store. There is a lot more choice of eco-friendly merchandise on the Internet—it would take days of driving to find the equivalent selection where you live.

DO YOU BITE? Ideal Bite is an eco-consumer service that emails daily sustainable shopping and living ideas. Friendly and charming, these tips are always wise, with a healthy dose of wit and not an ounce of judgment. And they'll link you up with great products and services (many are available in the United States only, but they are still very informative) to help you green your life a little bit more each day. Sign up for your free bites at www.idealbite.com.

Given the choice between driving your car to a mall to support a multinational company or buying from an entrepreneurial eco-conscious online retailer, I say shop online.

One of the best Canadian retailers for green products is Grassroots. They have two storefronts in Toronto, and a virtual storefront at www.grassrootsstore.com, for home and lifestyle options that are progressive and sustainable. Toronto-based Organic Lifestyle (www.organiclifestyle.com) and Rawganique (www.rawganique.com) are also reputable Canadian retailers with an excellent selection of eco-friendly goodies. Another good website for green shopping is www.pristineplanet.com—they act as an intermediary and connect you to producers of green merchandise (not all their companies will ship to Canada, but many do). A similar online retailer featuring exclusively eco-friendly clothing designs is www.greenloop.com. Quebeckers should pay a regular visit to www.ethiquette.ca, a site that reviews products and services for environmental and social responsibility.

#6 Avoid excess packaging

Why do they wrap the cauliflower in plastic? Or put the zucchini in a Styrofoam tray and Cellophane the whole thing? We can wash off the dust and grit from transported produce, but we can't remove residue from polyvinyl chloride (PVC) plastic.

How about watching kids open a new toy, peeling off layer after layer of Styrofoam, plastic, twist ties and cardboard, just to get at a little truck buried underneath it all? The wastefulness boggles the mind. Each Canadian throws away half a kilo of packaging *every day*.

Use your money to send a message. Don't buy products that are heavily packaged. Shop for produce at local markets where the farmers sell it like nature made it. Shop second hand for toys and children's clothes—the packaging is long gone! Shop in bulk and bring back your own containers to refill. Bulk buying can save you up to 50 percent on your shopping bill.

 ## Trip chain

No matter what you buy or where you buy it, if you are running out to the store in your car every day, you're making your mark on the earth. Trip chaining is simply a funky name for putting some organization into your errands so that you are taking care of several tasks in one outing and choosing the shortest route between stops. Not only will you save gas if you are driving, but you'll probably save time as well.

Your money, your power

You may feel like a helpless consumer with no power to change the will of the corporate giants, but don't forget you are the reason they stay in business. So let your concerns be heard by sending an email or a letter to head office if something they do bothers you. Be judicious about which companies you support with your hard-earned dollar. Pay attention to who is limiting packaging, paying fair wages and generally shrinking their business footprint. Check out www.climatecounts.org to see how serious various companies are about combating global warming, and to measure their performance against their competitors. You can even download a handy wallet card to carry with you for when you make your shopping decisions.

[15]
How to **Get Dressed**

Flipping through your favourite fashion magazine, noting all the "must-have" fashion lists for the coming season, you hear it: that little voice inside your head that cringes and squeaks, *Can't I just wear what's in my closet from last year? How much is this season going to cost me?*

There lurks, within all of us I believe, the voice of reason. Buying new clothes is not just expensive, but all the harvesting and manufacturing and bleaching and dying and transporting of all those must-haves are taking a serious toll on the environment.

Fortunately, being sustainably stylish is getting easier every season. The fashion industry, for all its vacuity, is deeply interested in keeping up with trends. And environmentalism is one trend that is on the rise. Here are the new rules of the fashion game.

 ## Be your own fashion icon

Ask anyone from Anna Wintour on down, and they all say the same thing: the truly fashionable set their own style. Don't be a slave to the machine, buying more new stuff every season just to keep up with some illusion of happiness sold on the magazine pages. Shop smart: invest in quality items you can wear for years, and jazz them up with your personal style.

#2 Wear organic

Cotton is the most heavily pesticide-sprayed crop in the world. Fully one-quarter of the world's insecticides are sprayed on cotton crops. It takes approximately half a pound of chemicals to grow enough cotton for one T-shirt. Your favourite white T-shirt could tell a dark tale if it could talk. Wait, it gets worse. Half of the pesticides used are classified as possible or known carcinogens. The good news is organic cotton is becoming more widely available. But it's important to be aware of how truly organic a product is, right down to the dyes and processing. And don't be fooled by the word "natural," either—it doesn't really mean anything. A blouse made of "all natural cotton" has been doused in all the same pesticides as a regular cotton blouse. Make sure any product you're considering is *certified organic*—which means it has been verified by an independent third party as meeting certain standards. Check out www.organicexchange.org for more information.

#3 Choose sustainable fibres

Bamboo, soy, hemp, and corn—they're not just for granola anymore! Alternative fibres have blossomed in popularity over the last few years. Cotton Ginny, Lululemon's line Oqoqo, and many other companies (see #9, below) are all making soft, comfortable and downright gorgeous fashions out of these unlikely materials. They're considered more sustainable because they're hardier plants and so require fewer or no pesticides to grow; the plants also regenerate in a short amount of time; and they make longer-lasting fabrics. But as with any new craze, approach these alternatives with cautious enthusiasm. Bamboo is a renewable plant with a very short growth cycle, and it's hardy enough not to need pesticides. It produces surprisingly stylish clothes, as do corn and soy. All good news, but the downside is that the plantations for these crops can displace native forests. And since it's early days for this trend, the fibre processing is, as yet, unregulated. But they're still more sustainable alternatives to polyester, acrylic and silk. And they feel so great against your skin, you may be tempted to eat them!

#4 Buy vintage clothing

Buying previously loved clothing is a fabulously earth-friendly way to look and feel great. And if vintage is fashionable enough to clothe celebrities on Oscar night, it should be good enough for the rest of us. Most cities in Canada have a second-hand clothing store or two—I bought my favourite winter coat, a 100 percent boiled wool Hudson's Bay parka, in Edmonton for only $33. Now that's a winner.

#5 Choose reclaimed materials

Reclaimed materials are increasingly being used in creative new ways. Both the ethic and the imagination of creating a second life out of old fibres rather than sending them to landfill are part of the appeal. The brilliant wardrobe designer at *The Gill Deacon Show* created a line of T-shirts for me to wear using old garments from Value Village. The T-shirts were so popular with celebrity guests that they all wanted to take one home. (You can too, from www.lusciousfunke.com.)

Stores like Preloved in Montreal and Toronto (www.preloved.ca), Nathalie-Roze in Toronto (www.nathalie-roze.com), Not Just Pretty in Victoria (www.notjustpretty.com), P'lovers in Halifax, Stratford and other locations in Ontario and Nova Scotia (www.plovers.net), and On & On in Montreal (www.onandon.ca) are the best go-to spots for brooches made from old bottlecaps, belts made from old hockey cards (you *know* I've got one of those) and clothing recycled into something new and fanciful. My favourite online site for imaginative recycling is www.eco-handbags.ca, which sells the coolest handbags on earth made from anything you can think of, plus a couple of things you can't. The One of a Kind craft show across Canada is another chance to connect with small-scale artists making the proverbial silk purse. The craftsmanship in reimagined clothing makes you feel you are wearing a work of art every day—each piece tells a story, each section of fabric comes from a previous life.

#6 Go for natural dyes

The textile industry creates a massive amount of waste, especially waste water. Most of that comes from the process of dying the fabrics. Look for clothing made with natural dyes. Roots now has a line of vegetable-dyed clothing and even leather goods. Ask before you buy, as not all their leather goods are vegetable dyed (www.roots.com).

#7 Rethink your clothes

Do I really need to tell you how much fun it is to have a bunch of girlfriends over for a clothes swap? You know what they say about trash and treasure.

Finding an excellent seamstress in your neighbourhood is another sure way to invent a new wardrobe out of an old one. I have successfully and very inexpensively repurposed old jackets as vests, turned dresses into skirts, and breathed new life into things that didn't used to fit right, all with the help of a good seamstress. If you're really feeling adventurous, you could even try doing it yourself.

Bag Borrow or Steal runs a website (www.bagborroworsteal.com) that lets you rent accessories for a monthly fee. You can feel "of the moment" without over-taxing the planet at your every whim.

#8 Avoid toxic dry cleaning

You pick up your clothes at the cleaners, throw them into the back of the car with your groceries, then drive around on a few other errands. Sound familiar? Okay, so here's the scare: traces of the known carcinogenic chemical per-chloroethylene—in solvents used by most dry cleaners—can be found in your foods by the time you get them home, *just from being in the car with your dry-cleaned clothes*. These are the same garments you put next to your skin. U.S. Environmental Protection Agency studies in the United States found perchloroethylene on the breath of people who had recently visited their dry cleaners where it was used. Greenpeace says that over a million people in the States are at risk from unsafe levels of this chemical in their homes. Scary, scary stuff.

Find a cleaner that uses silicone-based cleaning methods (such as Eco Cleaners in Toronto, www.ecocleaners.ca) or employs "wet cleaning."

In Canada, most cleaners selling themselves as environmentally friendly are false advertising. Only eight dry-cleaning outlets in the entire country actually fit the bill.

Garments are labelled "dry clean only" as a precaution, so you won't throw them in a hot dryer. Many of these items can be hand washed in cold water and hung to dry.

#9 Support enviro-friendly designers

Try to think of "mall" as a four-letter word. Whenever possible, support small, independent, ideally local designers. My favourites are the ones using reclaimed materials to create beautiful new clothes, like Susan Harris, On & On, Preloved and Luscious Funke (see #5, above).

Other great designers with an eye on the bigger picture include

- www.oqoqo.com (natural fibres line from Canadian yoga headquarters, Lululemon)
- www.twiceshy.com (funky designs from Vancouver)
- www.edunonline.com (Bono's wife's ethical and organic line)
- www.lindaloudermilk.com (luxury eco-wear made from self-sustaining plants)
- www.deborahlindquist.com (hip and gorgeous style from natural and recycled fabrics)
- www.ecoganik.com (leisure wear from California)
- www.thegreenloop.com (an online store selling only from eco-designers)

Some of the bigger brand names that are getting environmentally friendly are Cotton Ginny (they have several stylish lines made from soy, bamboo and corn), Mountain Equipment Co-Op (they've been selling organic materials and paying close attention to their suppliers' business practices for years) and American Apparel (they pay their workers fair wages, the clothing isn't made offshore *and* their business is solar powered).

For more info on just how dirty your favourite clothing companies are, check out www.sweatshopwatch.org and www.behindthelabel.org.

[16]
How to **Get Clean and Beautiful**

By the time she comes downstairs for breakfast dressed and ready to begin her day, the modern woman has spritzed, sudsed and slathered herself in more than 127 different chemicals. Most women try harder with every passing year to maintain a trace of youthful vigour and style. The terrifying thing is we may do so at our peril. Most of the creams and potions we depend on are made with an eerie number of mystery chemicals, many of which are more toxic than beautifying. Environmental Defence Canada's 2006 report *Polluted Nation, Toxic Families* found chilling evidence of high levels of hazardous chemicals in the blood of nearly every Canadian they tested.

THE SCARE:

Over 23,000 chemicals are registered for use in the Canadian market; about 300 new chemicals are added to that list every year. And in Canada, *industry is not required to prove that a chemical is safe before it makes its way into consumer products.*

Parabens: Methyl, ethyl, propyl and butyl—the wicked sisters—are widely used as preservatives in cosmetics. They can alter your hormones and possibly increase your risk for impaired fertility and skin problems. Studies have found parabens in breast tumours, though the source was not conclusively established.

MORE THAN SKIN DEEP Wondering how your favourite beauty products score in a toxicity test? Wonder no more. The Environmental Working Group in Washington, D.C., has done the exhaustive work to create Skin Deep, a database of every soap, shampoo, cosmetic or cream you could think of, with a toxicity rating for each one. Find it at www.cosmeticsdatabase.com.

Formaldehyde: Remember that stink from the frog dissections in high school biology? It's a suspected human carcinogen, and is thought to trigger asthma and eye rritation. It's been banned by the European Union (EU)— but here in North America, it's in your deodorant, nail polish, soap, shampoo and shaving cream.

Coal tar: Didn't think you were cleaning up with coal tar, did you? It was considered enough of a cancer risk to be banned from cosmetic use in 2004 by the EU, but in North America, you'll find coal tar (listed as FD & C colours) in shampoos, hair dyes and some popular children's bubble baths.

Lead: Not just for toys from China anymore, lead has been found in a range of common department and drugstore lipsticks, sometimes more than six times the FDA's recommended limit. Remember that lead was phased out of gasoline in the mid-1970s because it has been connected with infertility, miscarriage, organ damage and cancer.

Phthalates: You are probably well aware by now of how nasty those chemical plasticizers are. One called DEHP is classified as a probable human carcinogen, another called DEP can damage the DNA in adult male sperm. The extra scary feature of phthalates is that they like to move around, so though they may start on your skin as part of a fragrance, they can migrate through your body: phthalates have even been found in breast milk.

The good news is that in 2007, Canada introduced legislation that requires ingredients to be listed on personal care products. So now, as manufacturers slowly phase in new packaging and labels, you can at least be informed about which untested chemicals you're dousing yourself in. Empower yourself: for a complete list of the chemicals to avoid on your next trip to the drugstore, check out the "Dirty Dozen" list at www.searchforthecause.org.

In case you're thinking you have to go without altogether and avoid hygiene in order to avoid dangerous chemicals, fear not. Lots of fabulous products are available to keep you fresh and glowing the natural way. And the best news is they work. They'll even survive the unforgiving scrutiny of the television camera. I made sure that the makeup artist at *The Gill Deacon Show* used all-natural hair and cosmetic products on me and on our guests. She was skeptical at first, but once we toured the beauty section at the health food store, she discovered a whole range of natural beauty products that she now uses on all her clients.

Our guide to natural makeup and beauty products was Brian Dockal, an esthetician who specializes in holistic beauty and natural care products. Brian is part of the team at the Big Carrot, the largest worker-owned natural food market in Canada. If I'm ever wondering about whether to suds or scrub with this or that, Brian is the guy I turn to. I'll tell you what he tells me.

#1 Read the labels carefully

The skin is our largest and most porous organ, so it's really important to know what we're soaking it in and slathering on it. Take that extra 30 seconds to examine the fine print on the label. Look carefully for any of the nasty chemicals listed above.

And while more and more companies are willingly phasing out certain synthetic ingredients, they may not provide full disclosure on their packaging. A company's "proprietary blend" of essential oils could still be packed with phthalates, but you'll never see that on a label. Brian Dockal says that European legislation requires manufacturers to list any potential carcinogens on their packaging *and to label them as such*—a fairly effective deterrent for manufacturers to even use carcinogenic ingredients. If you're buying European-made products at a natural food store, you can be fairly sure they're 100 percent natural. Don't be fooled by products labelled as "natural," either—it doesn't mean a darn thing. Ingredient lists will always be your best bet for knowing exactly what you're buying.

#2 Be aware of what you put on your hair

There are so many types of shampoos available today that it's hard to know which is best not only for your hair, but also for your health and the earth. The general rule for shampoo is the fewer ingredients, the less likely you are to experience buildup.

One of the ingredients common to shampoos is sodium laureth (or lauryl) sulfate, sometimes listed as SLS. Not only has SLS long been suspected (though as yet not proven) to have links to cancer, but it is very harsh on hair, stripping the shaft of moisture, which means of course that you need to use more conditioner to remoisturize, then wash more frequently. SLS is a foaming agent—it helps work up a rich, foamy lather. But don't be fooled—the foamy suds are not what get your hair clean. Terressentials shampoo is clay based, basically the opposite of foam, and it works very well to get hair clean and shiny. Prairie Naturals, Druide and Ferlow Botanicals are popular Canadian-made shampoo and conditioner lines free of SLS.

Parabens are usually used as preservatives in hair products. Check the labels for these hormone-mimicking chemicals—Avalon Organics products have recently become paraben free. Be aware, though, that they now use food-grade potassium sorbate as a preservative instead, which some people like to avoid.

German manufacturers must label beauty care products containing parabens as carcinogenic—since no one wants to see *that* on their product label, most German-made hair products do not contain parabens.

If you are trying to wash that grey right out of your hair, you're going to have a hard time doing it without chemicals. There are some "natural" hair tints and dyes on the market, but you should really think of them as "less chemical." Naturcolor and Herbatint are two Italian-made products that have been around for years, and are ammonia and resorcinol free—the inside track tells me Herbatint lasts a little longer. For a chemical-free colour job, try henna, which is a natural tint that will condition and coat the hair with colour, though it is not as effective as dye for covering up the grey.

#3 Choose natural deodorant

You won't have anyone to get clean and beautiful for if you haven't got a good deodorant working. But nobody is worth smearing on toxins for, I don't care how cute they are. Let's walk through Odour Protection 101.

Antiperspirants use chemicals and minerals like aluminum to obstruct your pores so that perspiration cannot be released. If you think about millions of years of human evolution, you'll realize that perspiration is a necessary, albeit smelly, human bodily function. Sweat helps lower your body temperature and release toxins, so you don't want to lock it inside. What's more, aluminum has been found in the brain tissue of Alzheimer's patients, leading many people to wonder about a link between the two.

Deodorant, on the other hand, allows the perspiration to occur, but works to counteract any odour. It used to be that if you wanted to avoid the chemicals in most commercial deodorants, you had to avoid odour protection altogether. Now there are dozens of natural deodorants on the market—almost too many. It's easy to spend a lot of money trying to figure out which combination of natural ingredients works best for you. I know I've made the rounds of several different natural deodorant sticks—they seem to work brilliantly for a while, then like a capricious lover whose mood has changed, they stop working and leave you scratching your head as to why. I also discovered that natural deodorant is not necessarily chemical free. My one-time favourite "natural" odour protection contained propylene glycol, a petroleum derivative that is also used in antifreeze. Propylene glycol is used in a lot of stick deodorants to achieve that smooth glide across the delicate skin under your arm.

To be totally natural *and* odour free, look for crystal deodorant—literally a mineral crystal that you wet and rub under your arm. My running partner ran a half marathon with crystal deodorant. I huffed and puffed along beside her and didn't notice any undue stinkiness.

Another new product released in 2006 is called Dr. Mist, a mineral salt spray that kills odour-causing bacteria and is reported to work like a charm (www.drmist.ca). Druide and Green Beaver are popular Canadian-made natural deodorants that also contain no propylene glycol.

#4 Investigate your toothpaste

I must admit, it was not until I was knee-deep in the research for this book that it occurred to me: my organic-fed, walked-to-school, filtered-water children are brushing their teeth twice a day with brightly coloured fruit-flavoured commercial toothpaste. Upon further investigation, I realized that the artificial colourants, dyes and sweeteners that make those fun kiddie pastes are not only bad for kids' health, they're doing a real number on the earth.

Triclosan, the active antibacterial agent used in many commercial toothpastes (and deodorants and antibacterial soaps), is not as biodegradable as originally believed and has been found by researchers at Johns Hopkins Bloomberg School of Public Health to make its way into the water system, along with its chemical cousin triclocarban. When mixed with chlorinated drinking water, these chemicals create chloroform; when exposed to sunlight in water, they create dioxins. The other ingredient in many toothpastes is SLS, sodium lauryl (or laureth) sulfate. In toothpastes, SLS can cause canker sores, though some natural toothpaste companies like the popular Tom's of Maine claim it is harmless and still use it in their products.

Fluoride is added to many municipal drinking supplies in Canada, and while it certainly has been proven to improve overall dental hygiene, it has other less well-publicized implications. The head of Preventive Dentistry at the University of Toronto, who is also one of the leading consultants to the Canadian Dental Association (CDA), says that fluoride may be doing severe damage to our bones, teeth and overall health. The American Dental Association and the former head of the Canadian Association of Physicians for the Environment both say that baby formula should *never* be mixed with fluoridated tap water.

To avoid fluoride in your toothpaste—the CDA recommends *no fluoride* for children under age three—look for a natural brand like Jason, or those made by Canadian companies NewCo (lots of fun kid-friendly flavours) and Green Beaver (more adult flavours like coriander, mint and green apple). Tom's of Maine offers both fluoride and non-fluoride lines.

#5 Invest in natural face products

I've been trying to figure out the skin on my face since I was 13 years old. And while it's only getting more demanding with age, I think I have figured out one thing: the old adage "you get what you pay for" is especially true when it comes to skin care.

If you're going to avoid parabens anywhere on your body, make it your face. Parabens are more readily absorbed into the skin on your face, since you tend to apply face creams and moisturizers after a bath or shower when your pores are more open. Potassium sorbate is a food-grade preservative often used as a replacement for parabens. Some people go to great lengths to avoid it in food, so if you don't want to eat it, don't put it on your face. Logona, Lavera, and Dr. Hauschka are all popular— if pricey—European lines of 100 percent natural facial care, to suit a range of skin types. Dr. Hauschka products are made from natural ingredients grown right on the company compound in Germany, using biodynamic farming methods. That rigorous protection of quality standards is what you pay a premium for. Burt's Bees is a less expensive line that is also less natural. They use synthetic fragrances in most of their products.

#6 Check the ingredients in your makeup

If true beauty is more than skin deep, then I have some bad news: most makeup products contain some super-ugly chemicals that are being absorbed deeply into your body every day.

Many makeups contain talc. While you may associate talc with a clean baby's bottom, it is often contaminated with asbestos. Natural makeup products are all guaranteed to be asbestos free. Mineral oils listed as petrolatum or C-18 have been shown to clog pores and accumulate in heart tissue.

Parabens, used as preservatives, are also likely found in your favourite makeup. Trouble is, parabens are estrogenic, according to the U.S. National Institutes of Health, which means they mimic natural estrogen and can wreak havoc on your hormones. When your hormones are out of whack you can experience mood swings, irregular menstruation, skin irritation and other troubling symptoms. Parabens are also potentially carcinogenic.

While many makeup companies claim that parabens are a necessary evil, since preservative-free makeup would be impossible to manufacture, quality natural makeup companies belie that claim. By using pharmaceutical-grade equipment in an oxygen-free facility, companies like Dr. Hauschka, Lavera, Gabriel, Sante and Zuzu make long-lasting mineral makeup products that are paraben free. Lavera guarantees their products are stability tested and will last up to three years. Higher-quality factory conditions cost more to maintain than the addition of a cheap chemical preservative, so paraben-free products will often be more expensive, but well worth the investment.

If you're hesitant to convert all your favourite makeup products at once, lipstick and mascara are the best places to start. Recent reports of high lead content in lipstick are not the only reason to make you consider a pale pucker: aniline and tartrazin are likely carcinogens used to create colour; oxybenzone and cinnamates are synthetic sunscreens. They say that women ingest a third of a pound of lipstick every year, so you want to be sure you're paying attention to ingredients. Lavera claims their lipsticks are so natural, you could eat them straight from the tube. If you're worried about trading in gorgeous colour for a palette of nothing but earth tones, get over it.

Natural makeup gals looking for a high glam quotient have been known to call Zuzu the MAC of natural makeup for its amazing selection of vibrant colours.

Chemicals in mascara such as nickel, mercury and even formaldehyde have a direct pipeline to your body through your tear ducts; make sure that mascara at the bottom of your purse is natural.

Not all "natural" beauty products are paraben free: EcoBella still uses them as preservatives, and Avalon has just recently phased them out, so some older products will remain on store shelves. I'll say it again: check the labels.

Avoid perfume

When I was about 10, my mother developed such a sensitivity to perfume she could hardly go out in public, it gave her such instant crippling headaches. "Fragrance" is actually a blanket term for a whole whack of synthetic odours distilled from coal tar and petroleum, thrown together to create and secure a certain smell. The U.S Environmental Protection Agency found that 100 percent of perfumes contain the chemical toluene, which can cause liver, kidney and brain damage. Phthalates, some of which are known human carcinogens, are used to fix the fragrance in perfume to make it last longer. To a lot of people, fragrances are more like fumes; most of Halifax has been proudly scent free since 1999.

While individual sensitivities may vary, most sensitive noses will react favourably to more natural ingredients. Try wearing essential oils mixed in organic grain alcohol. Companies like Aubrey Organics and Essential Botanicals make natural scents this way using only plant-based ingredients. But remember, natural scents won't last as long as synthetic—if you're still smelling your perfume after eight hours, chances are it contains some of those stabilizing phthalates.

Another way to wear a favourite scent is to mix a few drops of essential oil into a neutral, scent-free oil (jojoba or sweet almond oil, for example) and rub it on as moisturizer when you step out of the shower. You don't even need to towel off—your body will absorb that moisture as it soaks up the oils. So you get fragrance and moisturizer in a single, chemical-free step.

#8 Be aware of what's in your nail polish

You're probably choosing your nail polish based on colour alone, right? Something to brighten up the tootsies after a long cold winter buried in boots. But if the powerful smell that fills the room after you paint your nails isn't warning enough, let me make it clear that nail polish is *loaded* with chemicals. The long list of toxic chemicals includes nitrocellulose (highly flammable, also used to make dynamite), toluene (a petroleum by-product that can affect memory and vision when inhaled even in low doses), formaldehyde (a possible human carcinogen and skin irritant that also causes smog), triphenyl phosphate (a neurotoxin with reproductive toxicity), and dibutyl phthalate (to prevent chipping, also used in tool handles and industrial signs).

Pretty pinkies just cannot be had without a few chemicals, but there are some better options. Suncoat is a Canadian-made polish that is water based, which makes a great choice for the kiddies in your life who want to play dress-up without a chemical soak. Water base notwithstanding, it can be really hard to get off, so it comes with its own corn- and soy-based polish remover. For a polish that goes on and off more like the regular kind, try No Miss or Sante, available at natural food stores, or L'Oréal Paris Jet-Set Quick Dry Nail Enamel, available at the drugstore—they're made without formaldehyde, toluene or dibutyl phthalate.

Here are a few of my personal favourite products, TV tried and tested:

Hair: Giovanni Organics 50:50 shampoo and conditioner, followed (on a good day) by Jason's Citrus and Mandarin Wax Pomade.

Face wash: They say that once you reach a certain age your skin likes to be exfoliated in the morning and washed gently at night. I use Earth Science Apricot Facial Scrub every morning and CoQ10 gentle foaming cleanser at night. Both are very affordable natural products.

Skin toner: The woman in the cosmetics department at my neighbourhood health store told me she swears by essential oil of rosewater for a moisturizing facial spray. Her skin is like porcelain, perfect and radiant, so in the vain hope of getting some of that smooth glow, I immediately bought a bottle. No porcelain skin here yet, but the smell and fresh feel are more than enough to make me happy.

Face cream: I'm a big fan of Dr. Hauschka's Rose Day Cream and get regular compliments on how nice it smells.

Body lotion: Pangaea Organics rose and lime lotion smells great and also has biodegradable packaging.

Lips: I'm not much of a lipstick woman anymore since I discovered Burt's Bees tinted lip gloss—100 percent natural ingredients mean I can eat it all I like.

ENVIRONMENTAL LINKS TO BREAST CANCER
If you're interested in learning more about the environmental and chemical links to cancer, check out two powerful Canadian films on the subject. Critically acclaimed NFB film *Toxic Trespass* (2007) and the award-winning *Exposure: Environmental Links to Breast Cancer* (1998) are both riveting documentaries. Olivia Newton-John hosted the film *Exposure* after her own ordeal with breast cancer.

[17]
How to **Take a Shower**

Take a shower, have a shower, call it what you like. A daily wash under warm running water is a massive demand on your hot water tank—more than 11 percent of our total energy consumption in Canada comes from heating water. No one's suggesting you give up personal hygiene to save the earth—but it's easy to be smarter about how you wash up.

#1 Install a low-flow showerhead

One afternoon a couple of years ago, I opened my front door to find a friendly young man standing on my porch. He was holding a cream-coloured chunk of plastic about the size of a fist, with a bit of metal pipe sticking out one end. "Here you go, ma'am," he said. "Your new low-flow showerhead." Before I could explain that there must be some mistake, I hadn't ordered this, he handed me the showerhead, along with a compact fluorescent light bulb and a section of insulating foam wrap for my hot water pipes.

Then, like the Pied Piper of Sustainability, he skipped off next door to offer my neighbour the very same pack of eco-goodies.

I'm still not exactly sure why that happened. I like to think that the friendly young man was a well-intentioned eco-millionaire, who wanted to tackle Canada's energy gluttony one household at a time. The more likely scenario, I think, is that my utility company was on an energy-savings awareness kick.

Whatever the genesis of the gizmo, we installed it the next day and it has been a brilliant addition to the household, improving our showers and saving us money ever since.

Low-flow showerheads are a marvel of science: they send out less water and make it feel like more. By mixing air with the water in the delivery nozzle, a low-flow head increases the water pressure. And for a family of four taking five-minute showers, a low-flow head can save you $250 every year. How do you know if you need one? If you can fill up a two-litre jug in less than 10 seconds, you've got an old showerhead. If the eco-millionaire hasn't rung your bell yet, grab a new one at your local hardware store and watch the savings trickle in.

 ## #2 Set a timer

Especially once you get a new low-flow showerhead with pressurized massage features, it's easy to get lulled into energy-hogging oblivion in a nice hot shower. But anything longer than five minutes is gluttony.

BRUSH UP ON SAVINGS They say the next Great War will be fought over water. With that chilling thought in mind, watch how many times you leave the tap running when you're not actually using the water. Once you become aware of your own wasteful habits, it's easier to create new, more sustainable ones. Turn off the tap while you brush your teeth. It's an easy way to start raising your consciousness, and saving on your water bill while you're at it. Teach your kids the habit now so their life-long pattern will be the right one.

Make it easy to discipline yourself—set a timer outside the shower. It's kind of fun to see if you can beat the timer. If you're used to long, leisurely showers, ease into shorter ones. Set the timer for one minute less each week until you get your routine so speedy and efficient you can do it in five minutes. (If you're a bath person rather than a shower person, you might want to reconsider that ritual. A five-minute shower uses 40 litres of water, a bath nearly twice that at 75 litres. So if you're really in need of some luxuriating in hot water, either fill the tub halfway or treat yourself to a soak just once a week.)

#3 Stop while you soap

With the flick of a switch, a flow adaptor lets you turn your water off while you lather up, shave and scrub. Then when you're ready to rinse, you turn the water back on again and you don't have to readjust temperature or water pressure.

If you can't find a flow adaptor, go navy style. Navy showers are the new rage in showering—they even have their own video on YouTube. With limited water supplies onboard navy vessels at sea, marines know to turn off the tap while they suds up. Try it on the mainland and watch how much you'll save on hot water heating.

#4 Check out the Power-Pipe

This device is pure genius. Designed and manufactured in Canada, the Power-Pipe is a drainwater heat-recovery system—a copper pipe that transfers heat from your waste water into your hot water tank, preheating your shower water. Don't worry, I don't understand it either. All we need to know is that it works, saves money on water-heating bills, and reduces a home's energy footprint—and it's available at Sears, Rona and the Home

Depot. You can also order one through the company's website at www.powerpipe.ca.

#5 Stop dripping taps

You might find that noise a little irritating as you're drifting off to sleep. And you may notice a bothersome rust stain where the drips land. But that's not the worst of it. A dripping faucet can really add up to a significant waste of water. The U.S. Geological Survey has a drip calculator on their website, so you can figure out exactly how much of the world's most precious resource you are personally wasting. Check out http://ga.water.usgs.gov/edu/sc4.html. Better yet, replace the washer yourself or call the plumber and stop the drip.

It will cost you a little more than a washer, but if you're serious about saving water in your home, a grey-water recycling device is a stroke of brilliance. When you think about how much of the water that comes out of our taps (and that we pay for) goes down the drain virtually unused, it really is like throwing money down the drain. The Brac system, made in Quebec, filters used water from your shower, bath and laundry and redirects it for use in toilet flushing or outdoor irrigation. Check out www.bracsystems.com and start your own revolution to stave off a water shortage.

#6 Use biodegradable soaps and shampoos

Your hair feels so good when it's freshly shampooed. It glows, it shines, and it infuses your most porous organ with carcinogens and hormone disruptors. Yes, most commercial shampoos actually contain stuff you wouldn't want to put on your car, never mind your scalp. Don't take it from me, check out the Skin Deep website at www.cosmeticsdatabase.org. There, the Environmental

Working Group has compiled a database of every cosmetic or beauty product you can think of, rated for toxicity. Yes, toxicity. Coal tar, parabens, propylene glycol and sodium laurel sulphate are just a few of the ingredients found in shampoos and personal cleaning products, and they have a disturbing list of health risks to go along with their foaming and shining properties. Since they aren't biodegradable, their ill effects carry on into the water system, long after they've left your bathtub. See Chapter 16, "How to Get Clean and Beautiful," for lots of fabulous earth-friendly options.

Look for vegetable-based soaps or glycerine soaps. Bar soaps mean much less packaging—it's easy to find biodegradable bar soaps anywhere from health stores to gift shops.

#7 Don't buy disposable razors

"Disposable" is a four-letter word when you're green for life, and disposable razors fall into this category too. Whether you are shaving your beard or your legs, a razor with replaceable blades is what you want to use, so you don't have to toss all those handles into a landfill—the EPA estimates that over 2 billion razors go into landfill every year in the United States alone. Recycline is an American company that turns old Stonyfield farm organic yogurt containers into razor handles for their Preserve Recyclable Razor. An elegant solution indeed. I've got some and they work exactly like any other razor and fit regular blades. Check out www.recycline.com to order, or ask for them at your drugstore or health food store.

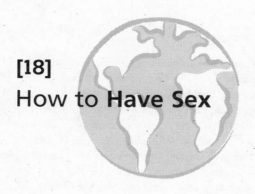

[18]
How to **Have Sex**

Did you turn to this chapter first? Were you hoping for some visual aids? I'm assuming that you're not looking to me for the actual mechanics of it all, just tips on how to give the earth a little more lovin' while you're at it—as it were.

The planet is certainly taking a massive hit from, as Bill Clinton might say, our sexual relations, and not just in the form of our bulging global population. As far as the earth is concerned, most of the trappings of modern lovemaking are more slap than tickle.

 ## Birth control

My husband and I joke that the hour before dinner at our house is like an ad for birth control. But birth control is really no laughing matter. Not only does our over-populated world need education about birth control, we need education about how to make earth-friendly choices.

The pill is heralded as one of the great scientific breakthroughs of the last millennium and a boon to the modern woman—I clearly remember my own feeling of empowerment when I began popping those little coloured discs out of all that plastic packaging. What I didn't know at the time was that all the hormones keeping my reproductive system in check were passing through me and into the water system every time I had to go to the bathroom. Whether from the pill, the patch or hormone injections, that synthetic estrogen makes its way into aquatic wildlife and has been shown to alter the apparent gender of fish, making male fish more feminized (intersex) and less interested in mating. In 1998, Environment Canada's nationwide study of sewage treatment effluent found levels of hormones and other medicinal pollutants—meaning your neighbour's birth control hormones just might end up in your tap water.

What about condoms? While nothing beats a condom for STD prevention and AIDS protection, they are a polluting menace to our water system. The Environment Agency of England and Wales estimates that between 60 and 100 million condoms are improperly disposed of every year in the UK. Don't flush used condoms down the toilet—they belong in the trash. (As a general water-saving rule, don't use your toilet as a garbage pail for anything!)

Latex condoms are the best and most commonly available option. Latex is made from the sap of the rubber tree, but the added lubricants mean they are not completely biodegradable.

If you or someone you love has an allergy to latex, you may be using polyurethane condoms, which are

---

THE NEXT BEST THING AFTER SEX Listen up, ladies. After sexual activity, the female urinary tract is especially vulnerable to infection. To avoid the decidedly unpleasant experience of a urinary tract infection—and the whopping round of antibiotics doctors tend to prescribe to get rid of one—make sure to pee right after sex. That little habit will save you a lot of discomfort, and keep those antibiotics out of the water stream.

essentially plastic and not biodegradable; they are also much less earth friendly to manufacture.

Lambskin condoms are reported by TreeHugger to be effective against pregnancy but not STDs, and they are completely biodegradable.

For longer-term sustainable birth control, you ladies can consider an intrauterine device, or IUD. It requires one trip to the doctor and a bit of discomfort to install, but after that the IUD is an earth-friendly, non-disposable solution. Be sure to get the copper IUD, which is naturally spermicidal, rather than the hormone-releasing kind.

#2 Natural lubricants

For those occasions when you need a little extra something to grease the wheels of your lovemaking machine, think carefully about just what it is you're smearing on. Those areas that can require lubrication are highly vascular— loaded with blood vessels connected to the rest of your bloodstream. Most drugstore lubricants are petroleum products; many contain artificial scents, flavours and colours. Look for products made using natural ingredients like aloe vera, grapefruit seed extract and vitamin E. Collective Wellbeing makes a glycerine-based natural lubricant called Good Glide, (www.collectivewellbeing.com); designed by gynecologists, Sensua! is a popular women's lubricant that is hypoallergenic, hormone free and latex compatible (www.sensua.com).

#3 Sex toys

I feel like a Puritan throwing cold water on a good time here, but I have to tell you, the pleasure gained from sex toys is hardly pure.

Most vibrators and dildos are made of plastic. To make the plastic softer and more like the real thing, phthalates are incorporated into the mix. Phthalates are endocrine-disrupting chemicals, confirmed by the U.S. Centers for Disease Control and Prevention (CDC) as toxic in animals. Because they don't bond with the plastic, phthalates have a tendency to migrate into our skin, mouths and mucous membranes; CDC studies found phthalates in 75 percent of their human test subjects.

The best bet for your next frolic is a glass dildo—no chemicals there. If you're worried about breakage in the throes of passion, surgical-grade silicone is sturdy, long lasting and dishwasher safe—if that is in fact where you wash your dildo.

If your pleasure toy of choice is a plug-in, opt for a rechargeable model or use rechargeable batteries.

#4 Natural candles

They set the mood, flicker flirtatiously and cast seductive shadows. Unfortunately, though, candles do a lot more than that. The majority of candles are made of paraffin wax derived from crude oil, putting even more demand on nonrenewable petroleum resources. *New Scientist* magazine explains that the carbon within that wax was originally trapped deep underground in oil deposits, and when those candles are burned the carbon is released into the atmosphere. Yes, your intimately lit love nest is contributing to global warming. Furthermore, Casanova, the soot from paraffin wax candles causes respiratory damage, scented candles are loaded with chemicals, *and* the wick you lit with such seductive aplomb is likely made with lead. Of course, you'd never really know, since

SAVE WHILE YOU'RE AT IT **Get into the habit of doing it in the dark—turning off the lights saves electricity. Showering together saves on water and probably soap.**

candle manufacturers are not required to disclose hazardous, toxic or carcinogenic compounds or to place warning labels on their products.

Let your love flame burn on a vegetable, beeswax or soy wax candle. These natural waxes burn longer, cleaner and more evenly than paraffin, without putting oily soot into the air. And they have little effect on the atmosphere since the carbon in plant-based oils was already in the atmosphere before it was absorbed by the plant. Undyed beeswax candles are best, in their natural honey colour. (Check the beeswax content—some "beeswax" candles still contain 49 percent paraffin wax.)

Check out Canadian-made environmentally friendly candles at www.burntoutsolutions.com and www.arbourshop.com.

#5 Feminine hygiene products

In the 1970s, manufacturers incorporated synthetic fibres into tampons to increase absorbency, which ultimately increased incidents of toxic shock syndrome. It was only in the mid-1990s that they stopped making chlorine-bleached tampons loaded with dioxins, when research revealed they release more than two hundred organochlorines. Most tampons sold in Canada are a mix of rayon and cotton. Conventional cotton is the most heavily pesticide-sprayed crop in the world; rayon is treated with chemicals to make the wood fibre derivative more absorbent.

Do the earth—and your nether region—a favour. Invest a few extra bucks a month in organic cotton tampons. Whitened using chlorine-free hydrogen peroxide and made from cotton grown without synthetic pesticides, organic tampons are a much safer natural choice.

But no matter what it's made of, your tampon and applicator still have to be disposed of. *E/The*

Environmental Magazine reports that 6.5 billion tampons and 13.5 billion sanitary pads, plus their packaging, wound up in U.S. landfills or sewers in 1998 alone. According to the Center for Marine Conservation, more than 170,000 tampon applicators were collected along U.S. shorelines in the same year.

To avoid disposal altogether, you could become a pioneer woman and strap a wad of cloth in between your legs; companies like the Canadian outfit Goddess Moon have made your job easier with reusable cloth pads. Lunapads and Many Moons Alternatives offer organic unbleached cotton options; Many Moons also takes the e-quotient up a notch by fashioning a line of reusable pads from leftover fabric scraps.

For my own solution, I must give credit to my friend Lisa. She ventured into the land of the refillable menstrual cup and has never looked back. A champion of her "keeper cup," she raved to me about how easy, cost-effective, eco-friendly and hassle-free her periods had become. Who can say all *that* about their monthly visit from Aunt Flo? So I waded into what I thought would be supremely unpleasant territory, all in the name of being green for life, and I must say I too have never looked back. The menstrual cup is the best thing to happen to the monthly cycle—ever. Buy it once, it lasts for 10 years; you'll never have to spend money on (or dispose of) another tampon or pad. Empty it two to four times in a 24-hour period, and practically forget it's in there.

The DivaCup is 100 percent hypoallergenic, latex-free medical grade silicone, and it's licensed as a medical device by Health Canada (www.divacup.com). Made in the United States, the Keeper (www.keeper.com) comes in either latex or silicone (the Moon Cup).

[19]
How to **Get Married**

For all the logistical and emotional headaches—and let's be honest, there are plenty of those—the union of two people in love is one of the most exciting celebrations in any culture.

When my mother was getting married in the 1960s, people measured a wedding's success by the amount of champagne that flowed or the amount of silk used in the bridal gown. Today, we measure the amount of carbon dioxide created by the average wedding celebration. And according to the UK offset company Climate Care, it amounts to a staggering 14.5 tons.

Of course, a lot has changed since our mothers were married. The church, the white dress and the diamond ring are no longer staples of the traditional wedding. Wedding planning has become so creative, the events themselves such personal statements that there are new traditions being created all the time. When my husband and I got married on a rock island in the Ottawa River which we paddled to by canoe, my mother pretty much thought the sky was falling because I chose not to wear shoes.

But (as I tried to explain to my mother), having a unique wedding that is a personal reflection of the bride and groom's values and style is practically *de rigueur*. And if sustainable living is one of your values, there are lots of ways to reflect that in your nuptials. It's getting easier and easier to bring your wedding's carbon count in at well under 14 tons.

The exciting thing is that whatever actions you take around your wedding will have a ripple effect—your guests will be intrigued, and ultimately inspired, by your choices.

 ## The invitations

You know a wedding invitation has arrived even before you open the envelope. It's the size of a legal brief and as thick as your morning toast with the inclusion of a reply card, return envelope, often a map and some requisite frilly paper items. A better alternative is to send wedding invitations by email. Now I know that sounds about as romantic as booking a corporate conference room for your honeymoon suite, but digital designers can help make your email as decorative as you wish. Create an email account where guests can RSVP; use Internet map software to direct guests to your location; send thank-you notes and photos by email. Ride the sustainable wave of e-communication and you'll save a few trees and more than a few dollars. Sending wedding correspondence by email gives you permission to send your thank-you notes that way too, which will save you time—and writer's cramp.

> **GET WITH THE PROGRAM** You're probably going to have to use paper if you need to print a program listing the order of service. Be sure to print it on recycled unbleached paper or an alternative like hemp or organic cotton. In both your choice of paper and the words you print on it, you can use the program to send a message, letting your guests know how important the environment is to you. Have someone collect the programs after the event for recycling.

If you are set on using paper invitations, be judicious with how much paper you really need to send. Since most regular paper is processed with chlorine bleach, which creates hazardous dioxins, choose recycled paper or eco-friendly alternatives. Glossy, metallic or plastic-coated papers seem to be popular for festive celebrations, but those kinds of treatments render the paper non-recyclable. Use matte paper, and ask your printer to do waterless printing using vegetable inks. When mailing paper invitations, use self-lick stamps instead of peel and stick adhesive ones, as the plastic sheeting they're stuck to is non-recyclable.

#2 The venue

In an interview on *The Gill Deacon Show*, the great climate change journalist George Monbiot, author of *Heat: How to Stop the Planet Burning*, said something that I'll never forget. In the "old morality" as he calls it, flying from London to Sydney to attend your cousin's wedding was a good thing. But in the wake of climate change and its attendant floods, forest fires and melting ice caps, there is a new morality, in which flying that far for a wedding is actually a bad thing.

It's tough stuff to think about, but it leads to some important questions to ask when choosing a location for your big day: How far will people have to come to join our celebration? How much driving or flying is going to take place because of us?

One way to alleviate any guilt over long-distance guest travel is to purchase carbon offsets. While it is by no means a remedy for bad behaviour, buying carbon offsets does have some value. The idea is that you pay an offsetting company to plant an appropriate number of trees to compensate for the amount of carbon put into the atmosphere by your (or in this case your guests') travel. Many airlines now offer carbon offsets with every flight, for a small fee on top of the ticket price. Remember though that any trees planted today won't reach maturity and full carbon-absorption potential for another 30 to 50 years. So it's not exactly an immediate solution to the problem. But you could argue it's better than doing nothing.

Another consideration around your choice of venue is decorating. A naturally beautiful setting will not only provide a stirring backdrop for the event, but will also require less money and effort.

#3 The flowers

Would you be horrified if I told you that most of the flowers for my wedding were picked from the ditch on the side of a county road? Not if I could show you the photos. Local wildflowers—especially when arranged with a skilled hand like my mother's—are as pretty as any imported exotic arrangement. The average cut flower

---

WHITE DRESS, GREEN POWER The lights, the sound system, the food prep, even the charging of all those camera batteries—it all adds up to a huge electricity bill for your big event. Since much of our electricity comes from oil- or coal-fired generating stations, every light we turn on contributes to global warming. But you don't need to sully your celebrations with planetary guilt. Arrange for your event to be sponsored by a green energy provider, such as Bullfrog Power in Alberta and Ontario (www.bullfrogpower.com). You can green power any event or meeting, or even power your home or business that way, to ensure that whatever amount of electricity you use will be put onto the grid by 100 percent clean and green alternative power sources, such as wind, solar and small hydro.

sold in North America has burned thousands of kilometres' worth of jet fuel to get here, and has been sprayed dozens of times with chemical fungicides, pesticides, growth hormones and chemical fertilizers. Many of the chemicals sprayed on flowers grown overseas are banned for use in Canada—and because they are not eaten, flowers are permitted to contain 10 to 100 times the chemical residue of foods grown in the same place.

Look for locally grown flowers for your wedding arrangements. Organic flowers will be chemical free, but local flowers have an even smaller ecological footprint. Of course as with all produce, if you can find them local *and* organic, you're away to the races. Eco Flora in Toronto (www.ecoflora.ca) and Amoda Flowers (www.amodaflowers.com) in Vancouver are florists specializing in local wildcrafted flowers and imported organic flowers that are fairly traded, ensuring that the workers who grew and picked them were not exploited or exposed to hazardous chemicals.

For table centrepieces, potted plants are a simple and affordable solution that won't be thrown away when the party is over, and they double as favours for your guests.

#4 The dress

Here comes the bride, all dressed in hemp? Absolutely. Alternative fabrics are cutting edge now in bridal wear, and for good reason. The fashion industry is one of the largest pollutants, complete with pesticides, bleaches, chemical dyes, sweatshops and child labour. Do you really want that legacy trailing behind you down the aisle?

If it takes a quarter pound of chemical pesticides to grow cotton for one T-shirt, imagine how much goes into a voluminous wedding dress. Choose organic cotton or another sustainable fabric for your dress. Pickering International is an eco-fabric supplier of hemp, organic cotton, soybean and bamboo fibres. White wedding dresses get that way from chlorine bleach, so choose the more natural off-white look. And support a local designer so you don't have to add long drives for dress fittings to your wedding stress list.

But perhaps the most eco-friendly approach to the wedding dress is also the most old-fashioned—wear your mother's. Vintage or handed-down dresses are a brilliant exercise in environmental stewardship. If your mother's dress isn't available, check out once-worn wedding dresses at www.thedressmarket.net.

For more on alternative fabrics and eco-chic fashion designers, see Chapter 15, "How to Get Dressed."

Something old, something new, something borrowed, something blue. Except for the colour specification, doesn't that sound a lot like reduce, reuse, recycle? Borrow whatever you can—the fewer one-use accessories you wear, the better. As hard as it may be to admit when you're in the excitement of the planning stage, your wedding is just one day—once it's over, life goes on. And you don't want to be left with a bunch of single-use wedding detritus that goes straight into the trash.

 ## #5 The ring

That unbroken circle is a lovely symbol of ongoing union. Unfortunately, the sparkly diamond and shiny

---

ECO TUX There's no doubt, strutting down the aisle in an unbleached hemp tuxedo would certainly make you feel like quite the sustainable groom. But if you're going to wear it only once, you're actually better off renting so you spare the earth the resources that go into making something new. A little known fact: the fourth R after reduce, reuse, recycle? Rent your tux.

gold are also symbols of exploitation and destruction. Awareness of the link between diamond mining and armed conflict in parts of Africa is no longer the preserve of the politically correct—it is mainstream. If you need more convincing, watch the Oscar-nominated movie *Blood Diamond*, starring Leonardo DiCaprio. In 2000, the United Nations General Assembly ruled unanimously on the role of the diamond industry in prolonging brutal wars and supporting violent rebel uprisings.

TreeHugger reports that as much as 15 percent of the world's diamond trade is in blood diamonds, so take a good look at the diamond you are considering and make sure you know where it came from. Do your homework and find a jeweller whose diamonds are certified by the Kimberley Process as being conflict-free. But even then, your diamond may have contributed to serious human rights violations, including child labour. Canadian-mined diamonds are positioned as being conflict-free, but there is a lot more to the story. The mining of precious gems and metals ravages the earth, often leaving a trail of destruction in its wake. Even in Canada, where environmental regulations for the mining industry are considered quite strong, the environmental degradation of drilling, road building and stripping vegetation for open-pit mines is enormous. According to the Boreal Forest Initiative, no one can sell a diamond, gold or any gem and say it was mined responsibly.

And that simple gold band comes with its own set of problems. The U.S. environmental group Earthworks says that the production of a single gold ring generates 20 tons of mine waste. According to greenKarat, purveyors of eco-responsible rings (www.greenkarat.com), 2500 tons of gold are mined each year, even though there is enough gold above ground to supply the jewel industry for the next half century.

So what's a suitor to do?

Probably the most green for life choice of wedding band is a family heirloom, if you have one. Giving new life to an old ring (from a vintage shop or antique market, if not your grandmother's jewel box) means no new energy was spent for your ring, so you're not directly supporting the mining industry.

Or you could choose a gem-free ring made from recycled metals; greenKarat showcases dozens of styles of recycled metal bands. For a list of retailers that support responsible gold mining, check out www.nodirtygold.org.

#6 The food

Feeding a wedding-size crowd is definitely a challenge (rubber chicken anyone?), especially for your wallet. But to make your wedding meal less of an earth-challenge, choose more sustainable fare. Organic food is certainly one of the healthiest choices you can make for feeding all of your favourite people. But organic food will often be more expensive, especially when feeding a crowd. (See Chapter 1, "How to Make Dinner," for more on eating organic.)

Buying locally grown food is not only one of the best ways to green any menu, it is also cheaper *and* tastier. Food that hasn't flown halfway around the world is fresher, treated with fewer chemicals and preservatives, picked when it's ready to be eaten, and just better tasting, plain and simple. Find a caterer who supports local (and, if possible, organic) farmers and suppliers. (One of TreeHugger's top-rated green caterers is Vert Catering in Toronto; check out their website at www.vert-catering.com.) For most of the typical wedding months in Canada (May through October), you'll have no shortage of local food supply. If you're determined to serve a certain dish, pick your wedding date based on when those ingredients are in season.

Although Canadians eat a lot of meat (twice the global average), more and more of us are turning to meatless meals. Serving vegetarian food, or at least some selections, is a wise environmental choice—see Chapter 1, "How to Make Dinner," for more on the earth assault of meat. Make sure your guests end their meal with coffee and chocolate that is organic and fairly traded.

Serve it all up on reusable plates and glasses instead of disposable. If your venue and style are more paper plate than crystal snifter, consider using potato starch plates, available through Green Shift (www.greenshift.ca). Their biodegradable napkins, plates and cutlery look exactly like paper or plastic but are made from vegetable resin that breaks down to compost in 43 days. The Barenaked Ladies and other bands are using potato starch plates and forks on their rock tours, so why not use them at your wedding?

 ## #7 The wine

I've never been much of an oenophile. In fact, I'm not exactly sure how to *pronounce* oenophile. While others may sniff, slosh and spit their way to a great vintage, I choose my wine based on geography. Everyone loves a cozy California merlot or a tangy Italian pinot grigio, but being flown halfway around the world to get to a Canadian table, those wines are soaked in petroleum. Buying local wine is an easy way to reduce your contribution to climate change, especially if you're buying enough to serve an entire wedding crowd. And the good news is that Canadian wines have come of age in spectacular fashion. Check out www.winesofcanada.com for information on local wines in your area, or get to know the local section at your neighbourhood liquor store.

Organic wines are becoming easier to find, but once again, your environmental score will be higher if you buy a non-organic vintage from your region of Canada than if you buy organic wine flown in from afar. Some tasty Canadian organic wines come from Frogpond Farm in Ontario (www.frogpondfarm.ca), Hainle Vineyards in the Okanagan (www.hainle.com), and Lotusland Vineyards, also in B.C. (www.lotuslandvineyards.com).

#8 The photographs

I'd bet good money there's not a single person reading this who hasn't been to a wedding where guest tables were outfitted with disposable cameras. They sure were popular for a while—I guess you can never have enough blurry drunken photos of the back of the groom's cousin's head. The good news is a huge percentage of those disposable cameras are reused and recycled. But a new trend is dawning. Why not relish the photographic possibilities of the digital age and put your guests' photos up on a photo-sharing site for all your friends to enjoy? When you set up an account on Flickr or Snapfish you can include

---

SUSTAINABLE SUDS For the beer drinkers in your crowd, serve up local brew. To find the beer that will travel the shortest distance to get to you, search the food and drink page at www.highwayhome.com for listings of every brewery across Canada. Only a few breweries in Canada and the United States are organic, as organic hops and barley malt can be difficult to source. Mill Street Brewery in Ontario and Pacific Western Brewing Company in B.C. are two popular brands to look for. Remember to order bottles not cans, as glass is much less energy intensive to create and, in the ultimate sustainable practice, bottles can be refilled. Aluminum cans must be recycled rather than refilled, and they are also much more energy intensive and polluting to produce.

captions (so everyone will know that the back of that head belongs to the groom's cousin).

Most couples still want to have a photo album of wedding pictures, but until you make the final selection of photos, keep it digital. Digital proofs mean you don't have to look through hundreds of shots that will be thrown out once final photos are ordered.

#9 The gifts and favours

In the Solomon Islands of the South Pacific, it is customary among the Malaitian tribe to give a thousand dolphin teeth to the groom as part of the bridal dowry. And while other cultures have different traditions of giving that may have a slightly less direct impact on the environment, the circulation of stuff at weddings is pretty universal. Guests shop for couple, couple shops for guests. Bride shops for bridesmaids, groom shops for ushers ... on and on the consumption goes.

Take time to evaluate what you really need and what you really want to pass along to your friends and family. Disposable plastic souvenirs are just a forgettable waste that drains your wallet and clogs up landfills. Give your guests something that keeps on giving. One of my favourites was a little bottle of local maple syrup with the couple's names on it. We thought of them over our morning pancakes for weeks. Other ideas for useful and meaningful favours include natural soaps, beeswax candles, regional food special to the area where you were married, bouquets of fresh or dried herbs, seeds in a commemorative container, organic fair trade chocolates. The Canadian company Plant a Memory (www.plantamemory.ca) offers place cards and note papers that you can plant to grow wildflowers, as well as plantable centrepieces and favours. The Sierra Club recommends a compact fluorescent light bulb for each guest, to counteract some of the carbon dioxide released by their car or plane travel to get to your big event. Or instead of a take-home favour, you could let your guests know you have donated a few dollars per guest to a charity or an environmental organization of your choice.

For brides and grooms, use this opportunity to acquire some highly coveted eco-friendly home products. Grassroots stores have recently added a gift registry to their website, for weddings, baby showers and holiday wish lists, available through their Toronto stores and their website (www.grassrootsstore.com).

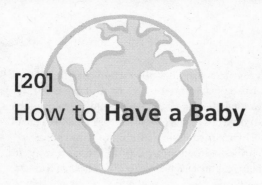

[20]
How to **Have a Baby**

There's nothing like having a baby to bring on unsolicited advice. From the moment a woman's belly begins to swell she becomes public property somehow, complete with uninvited touches to the tummy and wisdom on how to get through it all.

Well, getting through actually *having* the baby is up to you and Mother Nature. But for advice on how to keep your child as healthy as possible in our increasingly polluted world, you've come to the right place.

For me, having children was the tipping point for living a more sustainable life. That overused phrase "What kind of world are we leaving our children?" suddenly became crystal clear when I took on the responsibility for someone else's entire well-being. The great thing about greening your baby's life, in addition to how much of a head start it gives their health, is that you're creating a new citizen of sustainability, for whom eco-friendly living will always be the norm. Here are a few ways to make your little darling's carbon footprint as tiny and innocent as his newborn footprint.

#1 The chemical-free nursery

I remember my mother telling me I didn't need to fuss too much about prepping the perfect nursery before the baby arrived. "A boob and a drawer," she said, "is all a newborn really needs." I guess that means that when I was born I slept in a drawer.

But the woman has a point. Those matching bumper pads and hand-embroidered Roman blinds and teddy bears all in a row are really for us. Baby doesn't care if her carpet matches the paint on the walls; baby's developing lungs, brain and vital organs care whether the carpet, the paint and the bumper pads are off-gassing chemicals. And considering that infants spend about 95 percent of their lives indoors, according to the U.S. Environmental Protection Agency, it's pretty critical to think about what kind of air they're breathing.

New furniture and carpets, paint, air fresheners and even many baby care products often have a strong smell, right? That smell is a sign that volatile organic compounds (VOCs) are being released into the air. Common VOCs found in indoor air include formaldehyde, phenol, benzene, xylene and toluene—all suspected in a range of childhood health concerns. Most mattresses and furniture are made with polyurethane foam, which is given a honkin' dose of brominated flame retardants (BFRs) to keep it from catching fire. But BFR chemicals are part of the PBDE family: persistent chemicals that build up in human and animal tissue, and are considered toxic by Environment Canada. Ikea does not use these fire retardants in any of their mattresses or furniture; organic cotton bedding supplies for cribs are available at www.sagecreeknaturals.com and www.grassrootsstore.com. Willow Natural Home is a B.C. company that stocks every possible option for natural nursery gear, from bedding to rugs to bumper pads—check out www.willownaturalhome.com.

If you've already invested in a new synthetic mattress, be sure to let it air dry—preferably outdoors—for several days or weeks to allow more of the chemicals to off-gas before you bring it into the nursery. Tightly woven organic cotton mattress covers are a great way to seal up the chemicals (and dust mites) inside a vinyl-covered mattress, plus they are easily removable and machine washable.

See Chapter 10, "How to Decorate Your House," for more on natural paints and non-toxic furniture.

Then there's the business of swaddling, which usually involves soft cotton blankets in pastel shades. But remember that cotton is the most heavily pesticide-sprayed crop in the world. Picture what a third of a pound of sugar or flour looks like—now picture it as toxic chemicals. That's how much goes into the production of one non-organic T-shirt, perhaps one little blankie. Suddenly those pastel shades don't look so innocent. You just don't want your little critter wrapped in the same stuff we scrub off our apple skins, right? Choose organic cotton or natural wool fibres for baby clothing and bedding. Check out Vancouver-based Green Bean Baby (www.greenbeanbaby.ca) and Ontario-based Parenting By Nature (www.parentingbynature.com) for

GET READY TO START CLEANING There's nothing like a baby to turn your life upside down—including your shopping habits. We called our first-born "the baby who was bigger than a Volkswagen" because his arrival meant we had to invest in a bigger car—a little two-door hatchback no longer suited our lifestyle. The same goes for cleaning supplies—you may not mind the stink of chemical cleaning products yourself, but you wouldn't want Junior to take his first tentative crawl across a floor treated with toxins, would you? See Chapter 3, "How to Clean the Kitchen," for more on natural cleaning strategies and recipes for homemade baby-friendly cleansers. Because heaven knows you'll have more cleaning to do with a baby in the house.

a great selection of organic and unbleached natural baby bedding, towels and clothing.

Even if you pay no attention to the chemical content anywhere else in your home, go as natural as possible in the baby's room. Choose non-VOC paint for the walls, VOC-free glues and adhesives for any flooring you are putting down, PBDE-free mattresses and foam padding for bumpers, organic cotton sheets and natural fibre blankets.

Check out Chapter 10, "How to Decorate Your House," for more details on paint, carpeting and furniture. And get acquainted with the wonderful online resource the *Guide to Less Toxic Products*, put together by the Environmental Health Association of Nova Scotia. Along with this book, www.lesstoxicguide.ca will be a great guide to making your home chemical free.

#2 Diapers

The great debate—cloth or plastic? Well, you could argue that they're both bad, between the water and detergent used to clean cloth diapers, and the manufacturing and landfill accumulation attributed to disposables. But there are ways to lighten the load … on the earth, at least. The great green website TreeHugger (www.treehugger.com) says that cloth diapers have less than half the ecological footprint of disposables.

There is just no getting around it: if you're using disposable diapers, you are taking an understandable but highly polluting shortcut. Disposable diapers, for all their convenience at the user end (as it were) are immensely chemical heavy and resource heavy on the production end. And in the very end they clog up a landfill. According to Environment Canada, Canadians dump four million diapers into a landfill *every day*. Some studies suggest they'll be there for more than two hundred years before they begin to decompose.

In addition to filling up the landfill, diapers keep on soaking up water, thereby preventing rainwater from soaking into the ground where it's needed. Disposable diapers are made up of a plastic outer layer, all that super-absorbent stuff in the middle, and a liner that goes against baby's skin. One of the absorbent chemicals used is sodium polyacrylate, which can trigger allergic reactions, as stated by the *Guide to Less Toxic Products*. According to TreeHugger, some of those absorbent chemicals were banned in the 1980s in women's tampons but are still used in children's diapers. And those VOCs you're trying desperately to keep out of the nursery because they have been linked to cancer and brain damage? Well, don't look now but they're off-gassing from your disposables, according to a 1999 study by Anderson Laboratories in Massachusetts.

If the earth assault doesn't get you, and the health scare doesn't phase you, maybe the cost will. Consider that five thousand to seven thousand diaper changes are required, on average, in the first two years of a baby's life. (That number will be significantly higher if your baby is like every single one I've ever met—she won't be toilet-trained by age two.) That means it will cost $1500 to $3000 to keep a growing baby in disposable diapers, based on a rough estimation of $60 to $80 dollars a month for at least 24 months. Disposables keep wetness away from baby's bottom—which sounds great, but it means that it takes more time for a baby to process the discomfort of being wet. Environment Canada says cloth-diapered babies generally toilet train earlier than babies in disposables.

My husband and I spent $400 on diaper supplies before our first child was born. We bought 30 reusable unbleached cotton diapers and a handful of moisture barrier shells, all made by Mother-ease (www.mother-ease.com). They lasted through my first child's diaper years *and my second child's as well*; by the time the third one came along, a few became worn enough that they made better rags than diapers (but were they ever great rags). We supplemented with about a dozen more for our last year or two of diapering.

So, put down the calculator and check out any of the myriad natural baby product suppliers that have popped up since I had my first child in 1998; www.hipbaby.com, www.hankettes.com, www.mother-ease.com and www.parentingbynature.com are a few popular suggestions.

For all the benefits of cloth diapers without all the extra laundry, look for a cloth diaper service in your area. Diaper services launder in bulk, so the water and energy savings outweigh the impact of all the driving. (Just make

---

HOW TO WASH CLOTH DIAPERS Clean off as much of the diaper waste in the toilet as you can. Biodegradable flushable liners make this a heck of a lot easier.

Toss the rest into a diaper pail with a tight-fitting lid. Some people swear by filling that pail half full with water and hydrogen peroxide, or a water/vinegar/baking soda mix for soaking. I always found the pail too heavy to carry when I filled it with a soaking mix, but your arms may be stronger than mine.

Wash the load in warm water—twice a week is fine if you have a supply of at least two dozen cloth diapers. Vinegar in the rinse cycle will help remove any soap residue that could irritate baby's skin.

Line drying is best for the earth, and the cheapest and greenest way to get rid of any stains. Let the sun bleach them naturally. Otherwise, run the diapers in the dryer—with no skin-irritating chemical dryer sheets.

sure your delivery driver isn't idling outside your door during pickup and drop-off!)

For occasions when washing is not an option, such as that vacation at the cottage with no running water, choose better disposable alternatives. Seventh Generation and Tushies both make chemical-, chlorine- and fragrance-free diapers out of unbleached cotton and wood pulp. We found they were an excellent bet for those super-soggy overnights too. Look for them wherever natural products are sold.

#3 Wipes

If it's not the loaded diaper, it's the Magic Marker on your leather seats or the spit-up on your lapel. Yes, there's nothing like becoming a parent to get you hooked on those instant mess cleaners, hand washers, bottom wipers, the portable spill solvers best known as wipes. Although they are as taxing on the earth as the next one-use disposable product, wipes are no doubt very handy. The problem is, we get so caught up in their usefulness that we forget to pay attention to their ingredients and the effect they might be having on our children and on the earth.

A DIAPER-FREE BABY? Historically it's been the norm in India and China, and now a diaper-free movement is gaining attention in North America. It's based on the premise of elimination communication (EC) between parent and child, learning to read babies' body language and facial gestures when they are working up to something, then putting them on the toilet to do it.

See if it suits your lifestyle; find out more information and locate Canadian chapters at www.diaperfreebaby.org.

Most wipes contain propylene glycol, a derivative of natural gas, which is a nonrenewable resource. In 100 percent concentration, propylene glycol is better known as antifreeze. Scented wipes also contain parabens, the hormone-disrupting chemicals used to fix the fragrance and make it last longer. They're also bleached with chlorine for that sterile white look, but chlorine produces dioxins that are hugely toxic when released into the environment.

So for all their marketing about being soft and gentle for baby's delicate skin, every one of those commercial wipes is treated with hazardous chemicals.

At our house, we invested in a big pile of washcloths that we dampened with warm water for every diaper change. We'd throw the cloths into the diaper pail and wash the whole load a couple of times per week.

Greenpeace recommends reusable wipes from the B.C. company Hankettes; they sell a set of 10 reusable cloth wipes along with a natural cleaning solution (www.hankettes.com).

If you're hooked on the disposable wipe, at least modify your habit to lose the petrochemical soak. My

SOMETHING STINKS AND IT'S NOT THE BABY Take a good sniff of your baby products—creams, wipes, even the diaper bag you can't leave home without. A lot of baby-related products are now manufactured with perfume added. But when you think about the hormone-disrupting, cancer-causing phthalates used in fragrance and chemical scents, I'd take baby's natural smell—good or bad—any day. Choose products that are unscented or scented with natural ingredients. Check out Ottawa-based eco-retailer www.arbourshop.com or the Toronto shop Baby on the Hip (www.babyonthehip.ca) for natural and unscented products for mum and baby.

kids have been diaper free for years, but we still have a pouch of Seventh Generation Baby Wipes in the car for emergency spills and hand washes. They are unscented and alcohol and chlorine free, so they're not off-gassing in my car.

 ## #4 Bottles

When it comes to feeding a newborn, breast milk is the best for baby *and* for the earth. Breast milk comes with no packaging, so it creates no waste or pollution; it doesn't need to be mixed with water or heated. And, of course, it's free. So if at all possible, breastfeed whenever you can.

A night off is sometimes best for mum's sanity, so even a breastfed baby may take the occasional feed from a bottle.

But not all baby bottles are equally safe.

Many plastic baby bottles are made with polycarbonate plastic. Several studies, including some by the FDA, have found that polycarbonate plastic baby bottles releases a hormone-disrupting chemical called bisphenol A into the milk or formula during heating and sterilization. Studies at Nagasaki University in Japan found that used bottles leach nearly twice as much bisphenol A as new bottles.

FLUORIDE-FREE FORMULA If you are feeding formula to your baby, be sure to mix it only with filtered water. The head of Preventive Dentistry at the University of Toronto, who is a member of the Canadian Dental Association, says baby formula should *never* be mixed with tap water in a municipality where the water is fluoridated. Fluoride is actually toxic—that's why the dentist always insists that you rinse and spit, not swallow, after fluoride treatments.

Other plastic bottles, including the disposable bag liners used in some of them, have been shown to leach phthalates, another hormone-disrupting chemical, according to the Environmental Health Association of Nova Scotia.

Consumer Reports recommends parents *stop using any bottles made of polycarbonate plastic*. Since they are not labelled as such, either contact the manufacturer or just eliminate any clear, shiny plastic bottles.

Your best bet is a glass baby bottle with a silicone nipple. Evenflo makes glass bottles; Gerber, Playtex and Evenflo all make silicone nipples. Check out www.life-withoutplastic.com for these and other baby products, including non-plastic baby dining sets.

#5 Lotions and sunscreens

Baby's sensitive skin actually comes equipped with plenty of natural oils built in, so babies need a lot less product than we tend to slather on them. Avoiding soaps on young skin, or even bathing infants less frequently, allows those natural oils to keep a baby's skin healthy. For every little rash that comes along, remember that the more natural a product you treat it with, the less likely you are to irritate the skin further. Baby lotions and diaper ointments often contain any number of harmful ingredients, such as polyethylene glycol (PEG), parabens, ammonia, propylene glycol, coal tar, mineral oil and sodium lauryl sulfate. These ingredients have been linked to a number of irritations and allergies—parabens and other preservatives, for example, are one of the leading causes of contact dermatitis. Even lanolin, a natural oil from sheep's skin, is a common allergen as it is often contaminated with pesticides.

Vaseline is, as it clearly states on the label, petroleum jelly. Once you stop and think about smearing a baby's skin with a nonrenewable resource that powers the combustion engine, you might decide to use something else. Alba has a fabulous alternative called simply Un-Petroleum Jelly, made from pure plant oils and natural waxes.

Mineral oils like those commercial baby oils are petroleum products as well; mild oils (preferably organically grown) like sweet almond, jojoba, and even grapeseed are much more earth-friendly options for rubbing on your little ones. Aubrey Organics, Weleda and Logona all offer lines of gentle, natural skin care products for babies—check the labels, as some do contain lanolin. The Canadian-made Butterfly Weed line of lotions is made by two herbalists, and includes a nappy rash cream made with 100 percent organic or wildcrafted ingredients and even a belly balm for mum's overstretched skin after pregnancy. For extra-sensitive or allergy-prone skin, the German company Lavera has a neutral line of unscented baby products.

For newborn cradle cap, those oily yellow-coloured scales that can build up on a baby's head, the *Guide to Less Toxic Products* recommends massaging with pure olive oil and leaving it on for an hour before combing the scalp with a fine-toothed comb.

It's hard to believe that something as delicate and simple as baby powder could be anything but innocent to sprinkle on a tiny tush. But many commercial powders contain talc, perfume and dye. They pose such significant risks to a child's respiratory health that many pediatricians recommend parents avoid them. Talc is a mineral that is often contaminated with asbestos, making it carcinogenic when inhaled. For a natural powder to keep baby's bottom dry, use cornstarch or arrowroot powder instead.

If your pediatrician hasn't made it clear, the labels on

sunscreens will: do not use sunscreen on a baby under six months of age. New babies need to be kept out of the sun and covered in hats and long-sleeved clothing.

Once they are old enough to begin fighting the dreaded summer battle with you over sun protection, be careful to avoid chemical sunscreens. Check the label for any parabens (estrogen-mimicking chemicals used as preservatives) or PEG (polyethylene glycol, which opens up pores, making skin absorb other toxins more readily). Studies by the Swiss Institute of Pharmacology and Toxicology in 2001 show a link between synthetic (chemical) sunscreens and hormonal disturbances in the body.

The sad joke is that chemical sunscreens, in addition to being hazardous to your young child's long-term health, must be applied 30 minutes before sun exposure in order to work. So kids may get all those toxins *and* a sunburn. What you want for your baby's sun protection is a physical or mineral sunblock, which takes effect immediately; it sits on top of the skin and acts as a barrier, without being absorbed at all. The ingredients to look for in a physical sunscreen are zinc oxide or titanium oxide. Some popular mineral sunblocks are Lavera, Mexitan, Aubrey Organics and Badger. (The PABA listed as an ingredient on some natural sunscreens is derived

HOT SEAT **Hospitals won't let you take baby out the door without one, but the car seat is the latest locus of a chemical scare. In 2007 the Ecology Center in Michigan tested more than 60 different car seats and found one-third of them contained high levels of toxic chemicals such as bromine, chlorine and lead. These chemicals have been associated with a range of conditions, including learning impairment, liver disease and cancer. To investigate the environmental safety of your child's car seat, check out www.healthycar.org.**

from vitamin B and so is non-irritating; chemical PABA is highly allergenic.)

Beware of some baby products posing as natural. If you look carefully on the label of the California Baby sunscreen you'll notice the chemical polyaminopropyl biguanide, a derivative of (gulp) cyanide. Their proprietary blend of fragrance means it could contain pretty much anything, including phthalates, toxic chemicals used to stabilize a scent. The Environmental Working Group's cosmetic database, which ranks sunscreens and other beauty products for toxicity, gives California Baby's sunscreen a score of 1 out of 10, citing organ system toxicity and bioaccumulation as serious concerns.

Baby bedding

It's pretty much all you think about from the first night they're born. How can I get this tiny person to go to sleep so that I can do the same? Not to add another worry to the sleep-deprived new parent's list, but baby cribs and mattresses can be hot spots for chemical off-gassing. Many cribs are made of pressed wood, whose compounds are held together with formaldehyde, known to emit VOCs that cause asthma and contribute to ground-level ozone, or smog. The Canadian Partnership for Children's Health and the Environment says that VOCs from pressed wood products can persist in indoor air *for years*. Your best bet is solid wood furniture—several online manufacturers sell safety-certified cribs made from raw wood so you can finish the surface yourself with a natural treatment like linseed oil. Check out www.anaturalhome.com for some examples.

For more on avoiding the chemicals in polyurethane foam mattresses, treated with brominated flame retardants (BFRs) for good measure, see the mattress section in Chapter 21, "How to Raise Healthy Kids."

Toys

There's nothing like a baby to erase all the elegance from a living room. They may weigh less than a decent bag of groceries, but those little people sure do take up a lot of space. Floor mats, exersaucers, teething rings and stimulating toys—the kid clutter can be hazardous underfoot. Just don't let it be hazardous to your little one's health.

Avoid polyvinyl chloride (PVC) plastic toys at all costs. Though the toys may come in bright and cheery colours, PVC is the nastiest plastic of all; it is harmful to the earth and to human health through every stage of its existence, from the factory to our homes to landfill. When it is produced or burned, PVC releases cancer-causing dioxins, and communities surrounding these PVC facilities suffer significant groundwater and air pollution. To increase durability, PVC is treated with heavy metals like lead and cadmium, which are released on contact.

To create that chew-friendly softness for teething babies, PVC is mixed with phthalates—chemical plasticizers that disrupt hormones and have been linked to cancer. Greenpeace has been crying foul about PVC in children's toys for years; Health Canada recently took note and banned it from use in soothers and teething toys.

Ikea stopped making PVC toys over a decade ago, but most toys sold in Canada are made in Asian factories where PVC plastic is widely used. Better alternatives for teething and infant play are fabric and wood. Fabric teethers are phthalate, lead and cadmium free; if they're made from unbleached organic cotton, so much the better. To start your little one down the path to healthy eating, try the organic teething veggies—carrot, broccoli, eggplant and more—available at www.grassrootsstore.com. For a list of safe teething products, check out Health Canada's website at www.hc-sc.gc.ca. The five million stuffed animals keeping baby company in the crib may have friendly faces, but their material content is anything but. Most stuffed toys are made with synthetic nylon fluff, stuffed with pesticide-soaked cotton and treated with chemical flame retardants. Vancouver-based store the Good Planet Company (www.goodplanet.com) sells organic plush stuffed animals that are cute as can be.

Wooden toys made from sustainably harvested Canadian wood are a natural and sturdy alternative—just be sure they are treated with non-toxic paint, or untreated altogether. You can rub raw wood toys with linseed oil for a natural non-toxic finish. Grassroots also sells a line of wooden toys for young children.

 ### #8 Second-hand stuff

If you're just entering the baby stage it may be hard to imagine how you could ever come out the other side, but you will. And while you may miss those gurgles and coos, I can almost guarantee you will not miss having so much baby clutter around.

But in your delight at being free of the board books and bouncy chairs, don't go tossing them. Someone else out there could use what you no longer want.

There are lots of second-hand stores that will actually pay you to take that used baby stuff off your hands, provided it's in decent shape. Otherwise, donate it to a shelter or charity in your area. It's a great feeling to pass along something that has been part of your family's joy.

Of course, the most green for life approach to baby stuff is to acquire it that way too. Buying second hand means you lower the impact of packaging and manufacturing—and any off-gassing will likely already have happened, so it may be a healthier choice than new as well. I still buy most of my kids' clothing second hand at Value

Village and consignment shops—never be too proud to recycle.

Join the Freecycle community of recyclers and trade your old stuff for theirs in a virtual win-win. Freecycle has chapters in most communities across Canada, offering a free way to be green and pragmatic all at once (www.freecycle.org).

[21]
How to Raise Healthy Kids

When my husband and I were expecting our third child, everyone from family members to strangers on the street had the same comment, seeing us with our two older boys: *Oh, I bet you're hoping for a girl.*

And although the idea of soft girly things was an intriguing if foreign concept, our answer was always the same: as long as it's healthy, it doesn't matter.

Of course now we float along on an endless sea of hockey cards and bathroom humour, but at least our cabin mates are all in good health.

Every parent in the world has had the same nightmarish thought: What if something happens to my child? The idea of a child with a serious illness is unthinkable, unbearable for a parent to stomach.

It's what we spend most of the time doing from the minute we first hold their tiny folded little selves in our arms—trying to keep them safe and healthy.

So it's unnerving that the incidence of childhood asthma in some parts of North America has quadrupled in the past two decades; that food and environmental allergies are rampant among children in North America; that type 2 diabetes is no longer called adult-onset diabetes due to the rate at which it continues to emerge in children; that the proportion of obese children in Canada has tripled in the last 25 years.

The ways to keep our children as healthy as possible

are well within our reach, they just take a bit of extra attention on our part as parents. Once you've established a few new strategies for good health and a greener earth, you'll be thrilled by the results.

And as a bonus for your efforts, bear in mind that whatever green habits you create for your kids give back double to the planet; you're helping to improve the earth right now and also in the long run. By bringing up eco-savvy kids with a sense of environmental stewardship, we will leave the planet in capable hands.

#1 Choose organic food

It would be hard not to have noticed the increase in organic products over the last several years. According to a Datamonitor report, organic food sales have increased by 130 percent in the last five years. You may not be among the 85 percent of Canadians who say they have bought organic products before, but you might want to start if you have young children.

Nutritionists and health advocates agree that children should eat organic food whenever possible. Children are at an even greater risk from pesticides, because they eat more food relative to their body weight and because their little nervous systems are still under construction. Natural health researchers in the United States say that pesticide residues have been ranked among the top three environmental cancer risks by the U.S. government.

But buying organic doesn't always suit every grocery budget, so it's good to know where to prioritize. Milk and other dairy products are a good first choice for organics: many hazardous chemicals are bio-accumulative, which means they travel up the food chain. So the persistent pollutants stored in animal fat accumulate in us when we eat it—in the form of milk, butter and other yummy dairy products.

Children eat more fresh fruits and vegetables than adults (when was the last time you carried a cut-up apple around in your briefcase for snack time?) so it's important to choose organic whenever possible. For a guide to which produce is best to buy organic, see Chapter 1, "How to Make Dinner," or download the Environmental Working Group's wallet card listing the best choices for organic produce shopping at www.foodnews.org.

 ## Reduce their toxic exposure

Even if every last crumb that goes into their mouths is organic, you're still exposing your kids to dangerous chemicals inside your home. The disturbing truth is that all our houses are full of toxins, from our carpets to our cushions to our cookware. More than 75,000 synthetic chemicals have been developed and released into the environment since World War II. In Canada, industry is not required to prove that a chemical is safe for humans before it is brought to the marketplace—a surprising lack of oversight, especially when you consider the increase over the same time period in rates of chronic childhood conditions like allergies, asthma and neurological disorders like hyperactivity and ADD.

Toxicologists at Texas A&M University say that chemicals have replaced bacteria and viruses as the main threat to health, and that the diseases that have been killing us in the last several decades are of chemical origin. With that chilling thought in mind, let's see how we can take our health into our own hands and look for some serious chemical hazards to avoid wherever possible.

Lead

The summer of 2007 will be remembered by all for the news of lead found in children's toys—from that wide-eyed blue train Thomas the Tank Engine to the venerable

Fisher-Price and Mattel brands, recalls for leaded toys from China came down fast and furious. (Meanwhile, Greenpeace has been lamenting the lead content in plastic toys for years.) Also found in inexpensive jewellery and trinkets, lead can affect a child's aggression levels and lead to developmental delays and a lower IQ. Do you have lead water pipes? Have your water tested for lead, and use a filter.

So you can go through the jewellery box and the toy box—or shop for new toys—armed with the latest information, search for "lead in toys" at the U.S. Sierra Club's website, www.sierraclub.org. Health Canada and most news services have detailed information on lead concerns posted on their websites as well.

Polyvinyl chloride (PVC)

There is so much more plastic in your life once you have a child, isn't there? Sadly, most of it is PVC, which Greenpeace calls "the single most damaging" plastic of all. Lots of food packaging, plastic sandwich wraps, plastic cutlery and a terrifying number of children's toys all contain PVC. According to the World Health Organization's International Agency for Research on Cancer (IARC), vinyl chloride—the chemical used to make PVC—is a known human carcinogen. Many PVC toys also contain lead, but even the ones that don't are softened using phthalates—potential carcinogens and hormone disruptors. Phthalates don't bind to the plastic, so as soon as that plastic toy goes into a drooling mouth or even a clutching hand, the phthalates migrate: they have been found in human fat tissue and even in breast milk. The manufacture (and later disposal) of PVC creates dioxins, which are released into the air and water, enter the food chain, and accumulate in fatty tissue of humans and animals.

Ikea phased PVC and phthalates out of their toys over a decade ago; Chicco and Brio toys are also PVC free. Playmobil toys have been PVC free for 20 years. To check out Greenpeace USA's PVC report card for toy manufacturers, search "PVC and toys" at www.green-peace.org/usa. The area where kids play with their toys can affect their chemical exposure too—most vinyl sheet or tile flooring is PVC. (We've come to associate the word "vinyl" with "affordable," but we should really think of it as "toxic" instead.) Opt for natural fibres on your floors—bamboo, cork, hardwood or 100 percent wool rugs. Ikea is no longer using PVC in the manufacturing of their furniture or textiles. See Chapter 10, "How to Decorate Your House," for more on natural flooring.

Volatile Organic Compounds (VOCs)

VOCs are gases emitted from certain liquid or solid compounds—the biggest VOC culprits around the home are cleaning products. Some people get a headache right away from those strong fumes from disinfectants, bleaches, certain glues or permanent markers. But children's immune systems are less developed, so they don't always get the same warning cues from strong odours—in fact, many kids are drawn to them (try wrestling a Sharpie marker away from them).

For all the cleanups in your house—including the permanent marker all over the wall—use natural cleaning products, and whenever possible, open a window or door to improve ventilation when you clean. You'll find lots of details and recipes for natural cleaners throughout this book (see, for example, Chapter 3, "How to Clean the Kitchen," and Chapter 4, "How to Remove Stains").

Arsenic

Is your deck leaching arsenic? Up until 2004, pressure-treated wood sold in Canada—used for all the fun outdoor stuff in our lives, like decks, gazebos, fences, play structures and picnic tables—was treated with chromated copper arsenate (CCA). It is still used in play structures and picnic tables sold by many major retailers in the United States. So unless your outdoor wood fixtures were built recently with new wood, chances are arsenic is leaching into the surrounding soil and onto your skin when in contact. Health Canada recommends children wash their hands thoroughly after playing on any CCA wood play structures. If you're planning to replace your old CCA wood, remember not to burn it and release all those chemicals into the air! Treat it as household hazardous waste.

Instead of using chemical pressure treatments to protect outdoor wood from the elements, let Mother Nature be your guide on this one, and use cedar instead. Cedar is naturally weather resistant: a cedar fence or deck should last 30 years without much maintenance. And it smells like a walk in the forest—or perhaps a sauna—when it rains. I'm sure at this point you're thinking of throwing in the towel—it seems so overwhelming and terrifying, doesn't it? Where do you start? By taking out a second mortgage to fix all the chemical crises in your living environment? Don't worry, just take it one step (or one chapter of this book!) at a time. The Environmental Health Association of Nova Scotia has put together a brilliant and thorough resource for all kinds of healthy alternatives to toxins in your home. Bookmark the *Guide to Less Toxic Products* at www.lesstoxicguide.ca.

Walk to school

It doesn't matter how old you are, when your parents were children, they had to walk to school (and it was uphill both ways).

Older generations may be right to shake their heads at kids these days: gone are the days when a mother sent her child out the door to school holding hands with her sister. Studies show that fewer children are walking or biking to school than ever before. Other studies show obesity rates in children have tripled over the past 20 years. Coincidence? You decide.

According to Go for Green, an organization dedicated to active living, less than half of today's youth are active enough for healthy growth and development.

Walking to school is certainly the easiest and most reliable way to build exercise into a child's day, but it also has social and emotional benefits. A walk to school is time spent together: for a four-year-old, that is time to get familiar with the neighbourhood, feel the change of seasons first hand, see worms on rainy days and learn street safety. For a six-year-old, walking to school is a safe environment for downloading to a parent some of the social complications of the schoolyard; and for a nine-year-old it can be the last chance to keep holding mum or dad's hand before the pressure to be tough around peers takes over.

Some neighbourhoods or family schedules may not lend themselves as easily to walking to school—for those situations, there's the "walking school bus." Unless you live way across town from where your kids go to school, a walking school bus can help you get them there safely and on time, without you having to take them—it's like a car pool without the car!

It can be as simple as a couple of parents taking turns walking a group of neighbourhood kids to school, to something more structured involving scheduled pick-up and drop-off points. For more information and inspiration to join (or start) a walking school bus in your area, check out the Walking Tour of Canada (www.goforgreen.ca), where students can log the kilometres they have walked to and from school each day and track them as distance across Canada. Photos of happy kids walking to school together and testimonials from satisfied parents at www.walkingschoolbus.org will further your resolve.

October is International Walk to School Month—get started on a great enviro-friendly habit that can last throughout the year.

#4 Promote eco-schools

So they've walked to school after their homemade organic breakfast. What about the fumes they're breathing in from the synthetic carpet at circle time? Or from the chemical cleansers used to mop up the halls? Sometimes the smell from the industrial cleaning products in the janitor's closet is enough to knock you over—imagine what those chemical fumes are doing to the little lungs breathing them in every day. Not to mention the poor janitors—dried gum and spitballs are the least of their worries if they are cleaning with hazardous chemicals.

Find out about eco-cleaning products, available through many school boards. Inform your school care-taking staff that you'd like them to change the product request on their order—otherwise they may stick with their old habits.

Many school boards also have certification standards for eco-schools: bronze, silver and gold. Nothing like a little interschool competition to get the kids fired up about turning off lights and composting in the lunch-room. The future begins now, right here with those kids; get them informed about saving the planet they're going to inherit.

#5 Treat lice the natural way

Once your child has entered the school system, it doesn't take long before the notes start coming home about a case of pediculosis in the classroom. *Pediculosis humanus capitis*—more affectionately known as head lice.

I was mortified the first time my son had lice—thinking it was a sign of poor hygiene in our home. But lice actually prefer heads that are squeaky clean—natural oils on the hair shaft make it harder for their eggs to stick.

Yes, I have learned, it happens to almost everyone at some point—roughly 25 percent of school-aged kids get lice each year. But how you deal with your child's case of head lice is really important!

It's bad enough that conventional lice treatments—including the anti-lice shampoos available at the drugstore and recommended by some school boards—contain toxic chemicals including lindane. According to the Sierra Club, lindane has been banned in 18 countries, severely restricted in 10 others, and is the next candidate for fast-tracked elimination internationally. Lindane is an endocrine disruptor, can cause behavioural and learning problems, and can increase the risk of certain cancers. This is the same lindane found, along with other neurotoxins like pyrethrum and permethrin, in the many lice treatments sold on drugstore shelves across Canada. And if that isn't enough to make your blood boil, what makes it even more ridiculous is that these neurotoxic chemicals *have been proven to be ineffective at killing head lice.* A study conducted by the Harvard School of Public Health and the University of Miami School of Medicine has confirmed the failure of these ingredients to kill head lice. Worse still, the chemicals are actually the reason that lice are becoming more pernicious—they have developed resistance to the poison.

Pause here for stunned silence.

So no more commercial lice poison treatments or antilice shampoos. What to do instead? I have had three different cases of lice in my household over the past few years, and I can tell you that the non-toxic methods work brilliantly and safely to destroy those little crawlers.

Natural lice-killing techniques

Slather your child's hair—be sure to soak *all* the hair, which could be hard for you parents with long-haired daughters—in a greasy oil, such as olive oil, coconut oil or even a natural hair conditioner. Some people swear by a half-and-half mixture of vinegar and mineral oil—the vinegar disinfects, and the oil suffocates the lice. Leave it on overnight—send your child to bed wearing a shower cap.

Shampoo the hair clean in the morning, then comb through with a nit comb (available at drugstores, they are the finest-tooth comb you can imagine) to remove the eggs, or nits, from the base of the hair shaft.

You need to inspect the hair carefully every night before bed, for four to seven consecutive nights, to make sure no new nits have hatched. (Female lice lay eight eggs a day, which hatch in six to seven days, so you're not out of the woods for a while.) Repeat the overnight head slather if you see any further activity.

The Sierra Club also recommends using an enzyme-based shampoo, which would be labelled as containing protease, lipase, cellulase or amylase. These enzymes loosen the "glue" that attaches the nit to the hair shaft, thereby weakening it and making removal much easier. The lice produce those same enzymes naturally, so they will never develop resistance to them.

Throw your pillowcases and bedding into the dryer and run it on high heat for 20 minutes. Seal any stuffed animals inside a plastic bag for 48 hours—lice can't live longer than that without live food.

If this all sounds like way too much work for a busy working parent, there are nit pickers out there just dying to do the job for you—for a fee, of course. Look for a Lice Squad service in your area (www.licesquad.com).

Check out www.licebusters.ca for more on natural lice removal—Karen Tilley's struggle with lice has turned her into a one-woman crusade to stop the insanity around lice pesticide treatments.

#6 Use sunscreen the right way

From the day we take those tiny bundles out for their first walk, we cover them up from the sun. The skin cancer scare has us hanging all manner of blankets over their strollers and struggling to the point of near wrestling to get them slathered in sunscreen—I seem to remember to sunscreen my kids more often than I sunscreen myself! But sunscreen is not the whole answer; you need to be very careful about what *kind* of sunscreen you apply, and when you apply it.

In 2007 newspapers and websites were abuzz with research about the role of vitamin D in preventing a host of illnesses, including several forms of cancer. Most

---

BETTER BUBBLES There's almost nothing as cozy as wrapping your squishy little loveball in a towel, fresh from a bubble bath. What you can't see (but you can smell!) inside all those delightful bubbles are the chemicals used to make them so big and so scented. Phthalates (part of the "fragrance" ingredient), synthetic sodium laureth sulfate and coal tar (listed as FD & C) are just a few of the toxins your little bundle is soaking in. They can cause irritation of the skin and the urinary tract—it even says so on the label! Look for natural foaming bubble baths like Weleda or the Canadian-made Druide that will clean them up and leave them smelling sweet, without any hazardous chemicals.

doctors recommend that anyone living as far from the equator as we do in Canada should be taking vitamin D supplements in the non-summer months. Vitamin D is produced in the body as a response to natural sunlight. Even weak sunscreens (SPF 8) block the body's ability to generate vitamin D by 95 percent.

Most health professionals recommend 15 minutes a day in direct sunlight *before* applying sunscreen.

If you're using a commercial product from the drugstore shelf, it is most likely a chemical sunscreen; its ingredients are absorbed into the skin. Now, you're putting that on your little fella's skin based on the assumption that it contains safe ingredients, but remember, *there have been no long-term safety tests on the chemicals used in that sunscreen.*

Most chemical sunscreens contain parabens (methyl, ethyl, etc.), which accumulate in the body (they have been found in fat tissue and in breast milk) where they mimic estrogen and affect hormonal development. Studies by the Swiss Institute of Pharmacology and Toxicology in 2001 show a link between synthetic (chemical) sunscreens and hormonal disturbances in the body.

Polyethylene glycol is another ingredient that sounds like it should be in your windshield wiper fluid but is actually found in many chemical sunscreens, listed as "PEG" with a number beside it. PEG opens up the pores to absorb the chemical sun protection, but in so doing, opens those pores up to whatever other toxins may be present, stripping the skin of its natural immunity. The insulting irony of it all is that because they need to be absorbed into the skin, chemical sunscreens only begin to work roughly 30 minutes after they're applied. So your child may still get a burn—in spite of the chemical assault.

The best bet for sunscreen is a mineral or physical sunblock; the ingredients to look for are zinc oxide or titanium oxide. A physical sunblock sits on top of the skin, blocking the sun's rays from penetrating—so it works immediately, no advance application required. Some popular mineral sunblocks are Lavera, Mexitan, Aubrey Organics and Badger. (The PABA listed as an ingredient in some natural sunscreens is derived from vitamin B and so is non-irritating; chemical PABA is highly allergenic.)

#7 Avoid toxic bug repellent

With the spread of West Nile virus to North America several years ago, mosquito season just got even worse. But don't tempt one illness just to fend off another. Many bug repellents contain DEET, a chemical associated with neurotoxic effects in children. Some public health officials claim that products with 10 percent DEET or less are safe for limited use on children over the age of six months—though they clearly recommend looking for the lowest amount of DEET possible, and applying it no more than a couple of times per day.

Now that sounds like dancing on the edge of the dragon's jaws to me, so at our house we avoid using DEET altogether.

Products containing soybean oil or eucalyptus oil have been approved for use in Canada, and the Canadian Partnership for Children's Health and Environment (CPCHE) says that they are as effective as 10 percent DEET.

A lot of people swear by essential oils—the Internet is full of recipes for homemade mosquito repellent. The principle is to use volatile plant oils, and they work best in combination: lemongrass and cedar are popular ones, and lavender and geranium smell wonderful.

But even natural repellents are not without cautions: eucalyptus-based products should not be used on children under age three, and citronella products applied directly to the skin were discontinued in Canada in the fall of 2004. And you don't want to apply essential oils directly on the skin; mix them with an unscented natural oil like sweet almond or jojoba, 1 part essential oil to 10 parts almond/jojoba oil.

If you have any old sunscreen/bug repellent combination products lying around, *don't* use them—they have been banned. Toronto Public Health says they should be disposed of carefully at a household hazardous waste facility.

#8 Keep dust allergies under control

Dust mites are one of the most common childhood allergens. You may clean your house within an inch of its life, but you can't stop your skin from shedding in the night, and that is manna from heaven for the hundreds of thousands of dust mites living in your mattress and pillow. In addition to being supremely gross to look at under a microscope, dust mites can cause tremendous irritation for those with any sensitivities—and multiple sneezes mean lots of tissues, which mean lots of trees being cut down!

The easiest way to keep dust mites under control is to put a barrier around them—but *don't use a nylon or vinyl mattress cover*. Organic cotton bed covers, made of natural untreated fibres, are so tightly woven that dust mites can't pass through them—and organic cotton will survive a lot more washes (this is one load you'll want to use hot water for) than synthetics will. You can find them at www.obasan.ca, www.grassrootsstore.com or www.rawganique.com.

[22]
How to **Pack School Lunches**

Off they go into the big wide world, eating their lunch at school with their friends. It's enough to bring a lump to your throat—until you have to make those darn lunches every day, spend a fortune on lunch-friendly packaged goodies, and then empty out all the goopy, stinky remains of the half-eaten, unwrapped mess each night.

I can't help you with making the lunches every day, except to say that my nine-year-old makes his own and yours can too. But the crazy expense and horrible waste caused by all that packaged food and soiled wrapping? For that, ladies and gentlemen, we have solutions. We're going to avoid what I like to call the Three Sinister Ps of food: *prepared*, *processed* and *packaged*.

THE SCARE:
A school-age child with a disposable lunch generates roughly 30 kilograms of waste every school year. That's about 735 kilograms of waste each year from every class of 25 kids.

#1 Pack a litterless lunch

You've heard the buzzword from the PTA—litterless is the way to go with lunch. That simply means the wrapping and packaging from your child's lunch must be reusable. While this may sound like a whole lot of work to modify, let me incent you with a reminder of how much money you will save. Avoiding prepackaged, single-serving foods can save you more than $250 per person every school year. (Check out www.wastefreelunches.org for more how-to tips and a detailed price comparison between disposable and litterless lunches.)

Foods that are packaged and wrapped in individual portions (another Sinister P) are not only more expensive—you're paying for someone else to wrap your food—but they are as wasteful as they are convenient. Don't get caught up in the convenience.

Instead of Tetra Pak juice boxes, use a refillable bottle (see #2, below). Instead of prepackaged cheese and cracker dip 'n' spreads, fill a reusable container with some crackers and cheese cubes. Instead of a pouch with two cookies or bars, just put regular cookies into a Ziploc bag that your child brings home to be refilled the next day (Ziploc products are now phthalate free).

This is not rocket science. You can do this. And remember, it will save you money.

 ## Choose non-plastic refillable drink containers

It was only a few years ago that we were hit by what I call the Nalgene storm. In a bid to do right by the

---

SCHOOL LUNCH RULES Use: cloth napkins, Thermoses, stainless steel cutlery, refillable containers and bottles, lunch boxes or bags. (Vinyl lunch bags often contain lead; if it isn't labelled lead free, think about replacing it. Metal ones take a whack of energy to produce. Check out www.grassrootsstore.com for unbleached cotton lunch bags.) Avoid: paper napkins, plastic cutlery, juice boxes, paper lunch bags, individually packaged foods.

environment and save the world's oceans from a sickening glut of plastic water bottles, we seized on Nalgene bottles as a chirpy, colourful, reusable solution and a cool accessory to boot. Anyone who had a healthy exercise regimen—or at least wanted to look like they did—wouldn't leave home without a brightly coloured, virtually indestructible plastic refillable drinking bottle. Nalgene bottle knock-offs soon began appearing everywhere from Canadian Tire to Mountain Equipment Co-op.

But that was before we knew so much about the dangers of plastic leaching into our water—before bisphenol A, a chemical used in making those hard plastic bottles, became the subject of documentaries and investigative newspaper features, and before Mountain Equipment Co-op officially pulled every plastic bottle from their store shelves.

A refillable water bottle is still your best bet, but now the materials of choice are coated aluminum and stainless steel.

The Swiss company Sigg is leading the trend with a line of aluminum bottles in various sizes that are both lightweight and durable. An FDA-approved coating on the inside of the bottle ensures the aluminum doesn't leach into your water, but it may crack if the bottle gets dented. Check out www.mysigg.com.

Klean Kanteen is another hip bottle of choice, made entirely of lightweight stainless steel, a safe, inert and durable material. The bottles come in a variety of sizes, all with conveniently wide openings for easy filling and washing. They keep drinks cooler for longer. Check out www.kleankanteen.com for details; to order in Canada, go to www.lifewithoutplastic.com or www.grassrootsstore.com.

Mountain Equipment Co-op also has a line of stainless steel drink containers—perfect for adults too, some are even tapered to fit in your car's cup holder.

#3 Make your refillable containers last

You already know the major players in the refillables game: Tupperware, Rubbermaid and Snapware—they all have lines of plastic tubs with various lid mechanisms to prevent spills, and they stack for easy storage. Choose tubs based on plastic quality, not size or shape. Tupperware, Ziploc and GladWare tubs are now polyvinyl chloride (PVC) and phthalate free.

Make sure your child knows to treat them with care to prolong their life. Here's what you need to know about looking after them.

Wash your plastic containers by hand, not in the dishwasher. Many plastics contain phthalates, which can begin to break down when exposed to heat and leach into the water. For the same reason, never put hot food into plastic containers. For soups and other hot lunches, invest in a stainless steel Thermos.

As for baggies, the resealable ones are easiest to wash and reuse so you can squeeze a longer life out of them. Ziploc baggies are now made without phthalates. You'll pay a few extra cents for the name-brand zip-up bags, but the plastic is likely better quality and PVC free, and they will last longer.

#4 Get a modern Thermos

Fred Flintstone took one to work every day, so why shouldn't you or your child? Invest in a stainless steel, chemical-free Thermos (available at Canadian Tire and other hardware stores), and your kids can eat right out of the container—using stainless steel cutlery, of course.

#5 Be creative with wraps

My kids all want wraps for lunch now, like a sandwich in a tube. So now how do we wrap the wrap?

If you do package food in a plastic lock-top bag, make sure it comes home to be washed out and dried for reuse. Like my mother's, my countertop is dotted with upside-down baggies all drying out for reuse.

I recently discovered recycled aluminum foil, made by If You Care environmentally friendly products (www.ifyoucare.com). Made with 100 percent recycled aluminum, it is manufactured using only 5 percent of the energy it takes to produce regular aluminum foil. And it feels good to be able to "close the loop" by buying something made from all those tin cans we put out for curbside recycling.

But my favourite new discovery is the nifty Wrap-N-Mat, a reusable mat that folds up around the sandwich for transport, and unfolds into a placemat for eating. It's made with a food-safe PEVA liner that wipes clean and is machine washable. (PEVA is about as green as plastics get, but if you are still concerned, wrap your food in biodegradable waxed paper first, then the Wrap-N-Mat.)

Check out www.reusablebags.com for these and lots of other ideas and products that will lighten your earth-load at lunchtime. At www.wrapnmat.com they'll even offer you a discount price if you buy in bulk for a school fundraiser.

 ## #6 Eat fresh

It's an old health argument, but it applies here too. Fresh organic fruits and vegetables make not only the healthiest meals for you and your family, but also the most litter free. A reusable container filled with cut-up carrots and celery or a piece of fresh fruit wrapped in a cloth napkin beats a Three Sinister P snack hands down every time.

If you think the effort you make to change the way your child eats lunch is too minor to effect change, too small a gesture in the face of massive environmental crisis, think of it this way: every cultural revolution begins with the slightest shift. Start your revolution tomorrow morning.

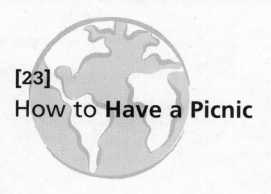

[23]
How to **Have a Picnic**

There's no better way to appreciate nature than to get right out there and be part of it. Breaking bread in the open air infuses a meal with adventure and a connection to the world around us, in a way that sitting at the kitchen table just cannot do. When the weather is fine and our pre-dinner moods are not, I have been known to assign everyone a carrying tote and trundle our entire meal over to the park. Eating outside somehow soothes the spirit—spills don't matter, children can run around mid-meal, and there are usually birds singing to put everything into perspective.

But how do you commune with nature without spoiling it while you're there?

#1 Litterless lunching

The golden rule of nature exploration hasn't changed since I learned it at camp as a child: take nothing but photographs, leave nothing but footprints. It goes for picnicking too. Whatever you take with you on your gourmet adventure, be sure to either eat or bring back home. Leave the park or the beach better than when you found it, so the next eager picnicker can enjoy it as you did.

The equipment

The basket

Get into the spirit with a wicker hamper or basket. For the serious picnicker, some picnic baskets come with reusable cutlery and plates.

The cooler

Double your enviro-pleasure with a funky picnic cooler bag made from recycled juice boxes that will keep your perishables as cool as your style. These jazzy-looking bags are handmade by a women's co-operative in the Philippines, out of juice boxes collected by local school-children. The kids learn environmental stewardship in their community, the women create a viable business to support themselves, waste gets diverted from landfill *and* your drinks stay cool. Win, win, win. Go to www.recycledplanet.ca.

The napkins and tablecloth

If you haven't already, now is the time to stop buying those bleached white paper napkins and disposable table-cloths. The disposable era is quickly coming to an end. Although convenient, those wipeable tablecloths are often made of polyvinyl chloride, better known as vinyl. Take note of that funny smell when you open them up for the first time. Who wants chlorine and toxic plasticizers ruining a perfectly good picnic? What you want is a nice old-fashioned cloth tablecloth that you can throw in the wash when you get home.

The cutlery

According to *The Green Book*, by Elizabeth Rogers and Thomas M. Kostigen, 40 billion plastic utensils are tossed into landfills every year in the United States—wow, that's a big takeout order. And they're made from polystyrene plastic, which you want on your picnic about as much as a colony of hungry ants. Styrene, which can leach from the plastic, is toxic to the brain and nervous system. Picnics don't call for your fanciest cutlery, just something a cut above plastic. Whenever some of our family cutlery falls victim to a kiddie construction project—which is to say the fork tines resemble a propeller and the spoon develops a neck not unlike a swan—I relegate them to the picnic basket.

The plates

Paper plates are a disaster—and not just when they collapse, spilling fresh raspberries down the front of your white T-shirt. We've been so long in peacetime, we've forgotten the old-fashioned war-baby logic of waste not, want not. Why spend good money on paper plates when you can bring your own and throw them in the dishwasher when you get home? If you're worried about breakage, Recycline makes a line of dishwasher-safe plates (and cutlery) called Preserve. They come in a variety of fun colours and are made using only recycled plastic (www.recycline.com). Or try a fabulous new alternative to plastic: bamboo plates are lightweight, take up little space, and are free of the chemicals that plastic plates leach into your food. Plus, bamboo is a self-generating plant that renews itself in just a few years, so it's great for everything from picnic plates to designer flooring (see Chapter 9) to T-shirts (see Chapter 14). Check out the plates (and a few T-shirts) at www.grassrootsstore.com.

The containers

You want your salad dressing on your salad, not your cookies. So you need properly sealed containers to transport your picnic foods. Choose your resealable containers wisely, as not all are created equal. Many of the plastic baggies and tubs are made using chemical plasticizers called phthalates, which do not actually bind with the plastic and so often migrate into the food. Many phthalates are hormone disruptors—not a tasty proposition.

Ziploc, Tupperware and GladWare make all of their products phthalate free. Be sure to take home your containers—and even your baggies!—to wash and reuse, so all the carbon impact of manufacturing them doesn't go to waste after just one use.

A brilliant invention for picnics is the Wrap-N-Mat. To avoid using so many of those darn petroleum-based plastic baggies or cellophane, wrap up your sandwiches and other small items in reusable Wrap-N-Mats. They double brilliantly as a food mat when they're opened up, and they're made of food-safe PEVA—which is as eco-friendly as plastic gets—so any spills wipe off easily. Check out www.reusablebags.com or www.wrapnmat.com for details.

The bottles

For toting your favourite beverage—which all depends on what kind of picnic this is, now doesn't it?—it's time to graduate to a stainless steel canister. Plastic is not something you want your food and drink sitting in: it's derived from petroleum, made using a heady cocktail of chemicals, many of which are known toxins, including phthalates (see above). According to the Pacific Institute, it took more than 17 million barrels of oil to produce the bottles used for bottled water consumption in 2006 in the United States alone. And that doesn't include the energy required for transportation. They also estimate that it takes three litres of water to produce one litre of bottled water. The total amount of energy required for every bottle is roughly equivalent to filling that plastic bottle one-quarter full of oil.

Whoa.

Back to stainless steel—it's durable, reusable, anti-microbial and stylish. Sigg bottles, with their trendy, colourful designs (www.sigg.com), are increasingly popular, although their narrow necks make for awfully tricky cleaning.

Klean Kanteen makes wider-necked bottles in a range of sizes, including extra large for that family picnic. See Chapter 22, "How to Pack School Lunches," for more, or check out www.kleankanteen.com or www.life-withoutplastic.com.

The mess

The last word on outdoor eating: there will always be sticky fingers, there will not always be a water supply. For portable cleanup jobs, disposable wipes really are a brilliant invention—except, of course, for the yucky chemicals they're soaked in and the waste they make when the wiping is done. Your truly virtuous choice would be to bring a dampened tea towel and a dry one. The Canadian company Hankettes makes a handy travel kit of 10 reusable organic cotton wipes with a refillable squirt bottle filled with an herbal cleansing liquid. Check out www.hankettes.com for more information. But for the less-perfect-and-organized—which is to say, those who are like me—there are unscented, alcohol-free and non-chlorine-bleached biodegradable wipes from Seventh Generation. Check them out at your local health food store, or at www.seventhgeneration.com.

[24]
How to **Throw a Child's Birthday Party**

Is it just me, or have you noticed that kids' birthday parties are taking on an insane level of fuss and indulgence? Gone are the days, it seems, when a homemade cake and a round or two of Pin the Tail on the Donkey were enough of a fiesta to satisfy kids. At what point did the child's birthday party become an exercise in keeping up with the Joneses and overconsumption? The culture of excess is one of the biggest challenges we have to contend with, so if we can start with our kids, and make them less gluttonous consumers, we're investing in a more sustainable future for all of us.

Birthdays are a good time, full of Kodak moments and more than a few stressors for mum and dad, but they don't have to put undue stress on the earth. Here are a few approaches to throwing a birthday party that have worked in my house and for a lot of families who don't want to blow the budget and the child's expectations on a store-bought megaparty. Just think, the money you'll save can go toward a nice bottle of red so you can raise a glass to another good year and heave a sigh of relief once it's all over.

 ### #1 The invitations

What's the point of spending money on those store-bought invites? If they don't get squished and wrecked at the bottom of the guest's knapsack, they'll be lost altogether.

If you really want a hard copy, try recycling old cards, magazine pages or colourful cardboard boxes into invitations. It's a great way to teach creative reuse of materials and include your child in the invitation process.

But to be most efficient and environmentally friendly, email is the way to go on invitations: save a tree by being paperless *and* get that information directly into the hands of the people who need to know about it: the parents with the calendar.

#2 The decorations

For all your festive decorations, buy once and enjoy often. Birthdays really are a family's way of celebrating the arrival of one of its members, so decorations can be shared among all family members. One-size happy birthday banner fits all, so you needn't buy a brand new one for each occasion. The same goes for table settings. A colourful cloth table cover and cloth napkins add festive charm, and they don't fell any trees in the process.

Unless you got talked into inviting the whole class to the party this year, reusable plates, glasses and cutlery are the way to go. No garbage, not much extra washing. (If you did fall for the whole class routine, renting is much less expensive than you might think, and those you don't have to wash.)

Latex balloons are just as much fun as mylar ones, but they won't keep the party going for years and years in a landfill. Latex balloons biodegrade within six months. So check the package or ask your local party store to carry latex balloons—the kids will never notice the difference. For the latex-allergic child, there are always colourful paper lanterns or homemade paper chains for recyclable party decorations.

#3 The cake

My kids have always loved homemade cakes—they get to choose the design *and* lick the beaters! I get a little grossed out by the artificial colourants, dyes and oil-based ingredients in those store-bought cakes. Just lick some of that icing off your finger and have a look at the oily residue that's left behind. That's because a lot of the artificial flavours in there come from petroleum. Mmm, mmm, good. Remember not too long ago when the top news story of the week was "Food Additives Make Kids Hyperactive"? The kids I know get plenty wound up on their own birthday party energy—they don't need synthetic additives to make it worse.

I've even been known to make a birthday cake for other people's kids, just so they can have a homemade cake. When you make 'em yourself, you know what's going in 'em, right? And little kids' bodies are still developing, so it's extra important that their building blocks be pesticide free. Relative to their body weight, kids eat more than adults—especially when it comes to birthday cake!—so use organic ingredients for baking.

If the idea of baking a homemade cake makes you want to throw every back issue of *Martha Stewart Living* right at my head, try Dr. Oetker organic cake mix. Delicious, organic and tastes like homemade. It's available in major grocery stores; check out www.oetker.ca.

#4 The ice cream

The cake just doesn't taste the same without it, right? Research actually shows that the fat molecules in milk and ice cream enhance the flavour of sweets on the tongue—so cake and ice cream at birthdays is basically biologically predetermined. Just make sure that those delicious fat molecules come from cows that were fed without synthetic additives, growth hormones, or chemical pesticides sprayed on their feed. Toxins are bio-accumulative (meaning they work their way up the food chain, becoming more pernicious with every step) and are stored in fat, so dairy products should definitely be organic.

#5 The candles

It's the moment everyone waits for—the moment your camera batteries usually decide to conk out—the lighting of the birthday candles for the ritual blowing out.

To make the ceremonial lighting emotionally *and* environmentally significant, be sure to light those candles with matches, not a disposable lighter. Worldwide, over 1.5 billion disposable lighters end up in landfills or incinerators every year. In spite of how handy they can be for the encore at a Neil Young concert, those little disposable lighters carry a big environmental weight: the casing is made of petroleum-based plastic, the butane fuel is a petroleum product. And how many have you found on beaches or in parking lots? Disposable lighters often wind up as litter.

Wood matches are made directly from trees, whereas most cardboard matches are made from recycled paper. So save a tree—light up with matches from a book, not a box.

#6 The gifts

Most kids I know are awash in toys—I know I have felt a little queasy watching my children tear through gifts at their birthday parties, hardly appreciating the contents of any one package, just moving on to the next one like a drunk on a binge. And I know I'm not the only mum who complains that kids hardly look after the toys they have.

If your kids are growing up thinking that their life's celebrations can be measured in material goods—well, they'd better get a good education because they're going to have a lot of expensive stuff to pay for when they're older!

Some parents I know say no gifts before three—kids under age three are too little to expect presents; balloons and cake are enough to make their day.

But once they get older and our culture of consumption has worked its way into their psyche, you can't just swoop in like a wicked witch with the official proclamation "No more toys at birthday parties! You'll collect food for the homeless—and do it with a smile on your face, young lady!"

That's what I call good intention, bad execution.

Birthdays can be an opportunity for learning, a chance to discuss material possessions and alternatives to consumption. Let your child be part of the solution to gift alternatives; maybe the choice of party style will guide you to other means of giving. A party at the fire station might involve giving gifts to families in need for the firefighters' annual gift drive; a party in the park might involve giving money to plant a tree in the community;

BOOKS FOR YOUR BUDDING GREEN FOR LIFER Two favourite books to give the little Green in your life are *The Lorax* and *The Gift of Nothing*.

The Lorax is full of the playful and whimsical language we love in all Dr. Seuss, but it's possibly as stern and dystopian as the good doctor ever gets. A poetic way to introduce environmental consciousness to your little reader.

The Gift of Nothing by Patrick McDonnell is a sweet, simple story that delivers a powerful message about the true meaning of giving. Told in delightful and simple words and pictures, it's a fantastic book for birthdays or holidays when kids can get giddy with consumption.

your little animal lover might like to raise funds to sponsor an animal at the local zoo. World Wildlife Fund Canada runs adoption programs—a donation buys you an adoption kit for an endangered species. Check out www.wwfcanada.org.

If you absolutely need to buy them something they can hold on to, there are ways to be more earth friendly with toys. Look for toys with less packaging, toys that are made locally, or toys made out of natural materials, not plastic. Keep yourself informed of lead content and other safety concerns with toys. Check out www.kidshealth.org for updated news on toy safety and recalls.

HELP LITTLE KIDS SEE THE BIG PICTURE If you've ever dreamed that your child might grow up and change the world, you'll remember who Craig Kielburger is—in the 1990s you could hardly turn on a newscast without seeing his young face, as his preteen shouts were heard round the world in defence of child rights and exploited child labourers. Craig founded Free the Children with a group of classmates in high school—today, with offices around the world, they build schools and educate children to help lift them out of a lifetime of underpaid labour.

Free the Children is an exciting organization to turn your kids on to, especially with their theme of "Me to We"—inspiring younger generations that caring about others is cool. Check out the Me to We section of the Free the Children website (www.freethechildren.com). There, you can join the Celebrate for Change campaign and receive a kit filled with colourful materials and resources to organize a truly memorable and inspirational birthday party. You could help change the lives of children around the world, including those at the party.

Give your electronics nut some rechargeable batteries and a recharger, explaining how much hazardous battery waste you'll be keeping out of landfill. For the game-addicted, check out the fantastic co-operative board games made by the Ontario company Family Pastimes, with strategies of play based on co-operation rather than competition. They have all the elements of risk, suspense and challenge, but force kids to work together to beat the odds or beat the clock. (The Secret Door is one of our all-time family favourites!) Check out www.familypastimes.com.

 ## The loot bags

The next time you're tearing across town in your mini-van, racing the clock to the dollar store for the last-minute ceremonial Cramming of the Loot Bags, consider this: the loot bag is an environmental nightmare.

Whether it's slimy string, glow-in-the-dark whistles, SpongeBob pencil erasers, racing cars, fairy wings, you name it—its life cycle is roughly as follows:

- made from polyvinyl chloride (PVC) plastic, petroleum-derived nylon, and other non-enviro-friendly compounds;

- assembled in a factory in China where workers are paid a pittance to inhale toxic paint fumes while they labour meticulously to get the dot exactly centred on the eye of that Spider-Man keychain (check out the award-winning Canadian film *Manufactured Landscapes* for a gorgeous illustration of the environmental calamities unfolding in factories all over China, all to serve the North American consumer habit, at www.mongrelmedia.ca);

- shipped halfway around the world by boat, train or plane at considerable expense to the atmosphere;
- pitched into the back seat of a gasoline-powered V6 minivan and driven across town;
- pulled from a loot bag by a tired, over-sugared youngster, played with once, twice at best, before being broken or lost, due to either shoddy quality or insignificance to child;
- deposited into garbage by exhausted parent (after child has finally come down off birthday cake sugar-high and gone to bed), fed up with kid clutter all over the house; then
- dumped into a landfill, neither biodegradable nor recyclable, nor really ever of much use at all.

Think I'm overstating it? Ask yourself, does your child even own, never mind play with, *anything* they have ever received in a loot bag? Does their interest in what comes out of those bags last *any* longer than the time it takes to get them home from the party in the car?

I rest my case.

So what do we do instead? How do we shift the culture and still satisfy the kids who have come to expect something at the end of Junior's party in return for all their frolicking?

The operative consideration here is some degree of permanence, or longer-term value. What is the message you are sending with your parting gift?

Some suggestions for loot bag alternatives

One clever friend found a chocolate maker in her neighbourhood who sold giant letters made of pure chocolate. So her most popular loot gift ever was a chocolate letter for every child—the first letter of the birthday girl's name. Another friend in Vancouver called up a few sports stores after Christmas and offered to take 16 junior hockey sticks off their hands if they sold them to her at cost, so her son's hockey party ended with each child getting his own hockey stick! Cost to mum: $6 a stick. Value and use to child: priceless.

Here are a few other loot bag ideas to keep the little ones—and the earth—happy:

- A packet of seeds and a little trowel for a spring or summer birthday
- Homemade cookies with the recipe written out on a card
- Custom-printed T-shirts with the birthday boy's name or a special design on the front
- Old books that no one in the house is reading anymore, which guests can choose from as they leave
- If he has outgrown his obsession, an older brother's hockey card collection, laid out for guests to choose from
- A custom-made CD of all the birthday girl's (or even the guests') favourite songs, along with a small instrument (recorder, harmonica, tambourine, shaker)
- A simple package of markers and pad of construction paper, as no house with children can ever have too many of those

[25]
How to **Celebrate**

Gathering with family or friends to mark a special occasion—it's the stuff of celebration in every culture on the map. But rather than being filled with earth-conscious choices, our festivities often rely on traditions that are either passed down through generations (think of that massive turkey on the Christmas table) or invented by powerful marketing forces (think of all those little paper Valentine's Day cards that kids give each other at school). Stop for a minute to think about how your approach to special events is affecting the earth. What kind of traditions would you like to start to create a culture of consideration in your family? If we all celebrate holidays in a sustainable way, we'll all have a lot more to celebrate for a long time to come.

 ## Halloween costumes

The most theatrical and child-centred holiday on the calendar, Halloween should really be my personal favourite. I still love to dress up, and I feel as close as I ever get to a domestic goddess when I stitch and glue my children's costumes together.

But I find the challenges of being healthy and sustainable to be more acute on this day than any other.

I confess that in the midst of writing this guide to making earth-friendly choices, I dashed out the night before Halloween to buy a wig for my son, to assuage his last-minute costume panic. No sooner had I opened the plastic package, excited to see how hilarious my six-year-old would look, than the entire family reeled back in horror from the smell of the chemicals off-gassing from that synthetic wig like a punch in the side of the head. My husband felt immediately sick and had to leave the room, and my son said the smell was too bad for him to even wear the darn thing.

I just got too consumed by the fervour of creative play and imaginative dress-up that makes Halloween such a magical time for children that I forgot my most basic abiding principles of shopping—buy natural, local and handmade if possible, and buy only what you need.

Well, I'm certainly learning along with the rest of the world.

So much of what we grab to use once for a Halloween costume is made in developing nations, out of petroleum-based ingredients like nylon and polyvinyl chloride (PVC) plastic. Many of the trinkets we adorn our little fairies and princesses with are made using lead, and many of the scary facemasks and wigs are off-gassing volatile organic compounds (VOCs) directly onto our children's skin and hair. Face painting beats a mask for creativity and health friendliness, but even non-toxic face paints contain chemicals you might not want absorbed into your little goblin's body.

FABULOUS FACES THAT WASH UP IN A SNAP
Mix together:
> 1 teaspoon cornstarch
> 1 teaspoon water
> 1 teaspoon organic/natural skin cream
> a few drops of food colouring

(It's not hard, trust me.)

Make or assemble Halloween costumes from used clothing—Goodwill, Value Village and other thrift shops are your best friend when the witches and goblins come out. For fabulous costumes made with fabric, not plastic, check out www.magiccabin.com. To support Canadian costume-makers creating mostly fabric-based designs, check out www.dreampowercostumes.com based in St. Jacob's, Ontario.

 #2 Halloween candy

Most parents I know love the lead up to Halloween (decorating, costumes and excited children) and hate the fallout (tantrums, cavities and hyperactivity). For years I thought the post-Halloween horrors of my children's behaviour was due to all the extra sugar and chocolate they were ingesting. But it's even more sinister than that. Acacia gum, used in gumdrops, toffee and M&M's to bind ingredients, is also found in postage stamps, paint and fireworks. Carnauba wax, which gives chocolate and candies a shiny coat, is also found in shoe polish, surfboard wax and mascara.

Certain dyes used to make those fun candy colours have been banned in many developed countries but are still in use in Canada and the United States.

Research from the U.S. Center for Science in the Public Interest (CSPI) states that products containing artificial dyes have had inadequate testing for human consumption and can be linked to a range of illnesses from allergic reactions to cancer. Many of the chemicals used to make those treats so tasty are neurotoxins—so my four-year-old isn't just oversugared when he's bouncing off the walls, he's actually hopped up on a chemical cocktail.

For a good time that won't make your trick-or-treaters part of a long-term chemistry experiment, there is—as oxymoronic as it sounds—organic candy. The Canadian company Pure Fun makes all manner of sweet treats using natural sweeteners like brown rice syrup and evaporated cane juice, and colourants derived from vegetables. As of early 2008, Pure Fun candies are now available in Canadian supermarkets. Other organic candy companies include RJ's all-natural licorice, GoNaturally Organic hard candies, and Seeds of Change, all available at health food stores. Or you can hand out the best-tasting chocolate on the block—fair trade organic Halloween mini bars from Cocoa Camino, available in bulk (www.cocoacamino.com).

 ## Holiday chocolate

From Valentine's Day to Easter and right on down the calendar to Halloween, chocolate is the holiday confection of choice. But there is a dark side to chocolate that might change your mind when you're thinking about

---

REVERSE TRICK-OR-TREATING Can you imagine a world where people didn't buy food harvested by children in slave labour conditions? Can you imagine teenagers putting down their trick-or-treating pillowcases and shelling out information to adults about the dangers of the cocoa industry instead? If neither scenario sounds all that plausible, take heart. Reverse trick-or-treating is an initiative of TransFair Canada and Engineers without Borders—going door-to-door in communities across Canada and the United States to educate consumers about fair trade chocolate. To find out more about fair trade chocolate, check out www.cocoacamino.com; for more on reverse trick-or-treating, check out www.globalexchange.org/campaigns/fairtrade/cocoa/reversetrickortreating/ca.

buying your next chocolate bar. As the demand for chocolate has increased, farmers have replaced native shade-grown beans with a high-yield plant of lower quality that requires industrial chemicals to grow. Cocoa is sprayed with organochlorines like lindane, which is banned in Canada and Europe, but not in the West African countries where the chocolate we eat in Canada comes from. Many of the workers applying those hazardous chemicals are children, forced into slave labour. Read *Bitter Chocolate* by Carol Off or visit the Global Exchange website (www.globalexchange.org)—both will forever change the way you view chocolate.

The solution is simple and delicious. Buy fair trade chocolate. Fair trade practices ensure that abusive child labour is prohibited, that farming families earn a living wage and that cocoa production is environmentally sustainable. Organic chocolate, while it will certainly be healthier to eat, is not necessarily fairly traded. Look for

THE ADVENT OF SOMETHING BETTER **Before Christmas one year, one of my boys was desperate for an advent calendar. He wanted to pop open a little plastic window and eat chocolate every day for the month of December, just like he had heard his friends were doing. But when I explained how conventional chocolate was grown, and how children like him were treated during the process, he agreed we should look for fair trade chocolate. A trip to Ten Thousand Villages, a non-profit organization that sells fairly traded handicrafts in shops across North America, saved the day. We found a bright red cotton refillable advent calendar made in India and fairly traded. We filled the pockets with fair trade chocolates ourselves (our leftover Halloween minis, actually) and created a new fair trade and garbage-free tradition in the process.**

Cocoa Camino organic fair trade products—including Halloween minis—from the co-operative La Siembra, Canada's largest fair trade chocolate company (www.cocoacamino.com).

#4 Christmas trees

Chopping down a live tree only to throw it away a couple of weeks later? That couldn't be the most environmental choice of Christmas tree, now could it?

Well, no, actually it's not. Decorating a houseplant or the tree on your front lawn would be the most environmental Christmas tree. But if you have to choose between cutting down a live tree and reusing an artificial one, the live Christmas tree wins.

I know you meticulously repackage those clip-on tree branches every January and reassemble them the following December. It seems like counterintuitive environmental logic to cut down an oxygen-producing tree instead.

But keep in mind that almost every tree in the artificial forest is made in China out of polyvinyl chloride (PVC). Greenpeace says PVC is the single most hideous plastic of them all. Vinyl chloride is a known carcinogen, and it creates hazardous dioxins during manufacturing and disposal. Most PVC products contain lead, used to stabilize the plastics, which is why artificial trees come with warning labels cautioning consumers not to inhale or ingest dust and residue from the branches.

A real tree, preferably one grown on a small family operation near where you live, is a much preferable option. For the few years it is alive, it absorbs some of the carbon dioxide emitted by all the planes bringing fake trees over from China. And it is certainly safe, if prickly, for children to touch or eat.

Christmas tree farms are typically large agricultural operations, so your tree may well have been sprayed with herbicides or pesticides during its short life. Smaller family businesses often have more sustainable growing practices—and smaller crowds in their U-pick sections.

Of course, if you never cut it down it can keep on growing until next Christmas. Potted Christmas trees can get all dressed up for festivity in your living room, then head back outdoors to be planted in the spring.

 ## #5 Holiday cards

Are you one of those organized people who send out holiday cards every year? I can never seem to find the time before about mid-January. Whenever you get around to it, if you want to be green for life, send your holiday wishes by email.

According to the Greeting Card Association, Americans spend $7.5 billion on greeting cards every year, and the holiday season makes up a considerable portion of those profits. When you consider that most of those cards are made from wood pulp, are chlorine bleached, and require the use of fossil fuels when they are delivered, greeting cards excise quite a toll on the earth.

E-cards are festive, personal and paperless. They are delivered virtually, with no carbon cost. The E-Cards

---

BE BRIGHT ABOUT HOLIDAY LIGHTS The thought of twinkling lights under a blanket of fresh snow can make you feel all warm inside. But electricity from coal-fired plants is a major contributor to global warming, so make sure your outdoor lights—and tree lights—are LED. The light-emitting diode technology uses 95 percent less energy than an incandescent bulb. If you set up a timer so your lights won't be on all night, you'll use even less. That way your festive lighting won't take such a toll on the earth or your electricity bill.

company offers dozens of custom options for cards, and they donate part of their profits to wildlife conservation organizations, including the World Wildlife Fund (www.e-cards.com). Perhaps the most magical e-cards ever are made by graphic UK artist Jacquie Lawson. I eagerly await finding these animated musical greetings in my inbox every December (www.jacquielawson.com).

If pen to page is still your favourite way to communicate, remember that your choice of greeting card sends as powerful a message as what's written inside. Look for cards made from recycled paper, organic cotton or hemp. Paporganics makes tree-free organic cotton holiday gift card packs (www.paporganics.com); Global Exchange sells fair trade holiday cards made in Nepal from sustainably harvested materials (www.gxonlinestore.org).

Buying UNICEF cards helps support health and education programs for children in need around the world (www.shopunicef.ca).

#6 Gift wrap

That adorable roll of holiday wrap you bought on sale last January may not seem like a big deal, but you should know that wrapping paper is an environmental menace. According to TreeHugger, 83 million square metres of gift wrap gets thrown away after every holiday season in the UK alone.

While it may look pretty under the tree or at the birthday party, the wrapping paper isn't what that special someone really cares about. Who remembers what their gifts were wrapped in anyway? At our house, we save as much wrapping paper as we can each Christmas and reuse it the following year. And the year after that.

You can order tree-free gift wrap, made from hemp and flax, through the Good Planet Company store in Victoria (www.goodplanet.com). Paporganics sells a line of wrap made from 90 percent postconsumer fibre and 10 percent hemp (www.paporganics.com).

Some creative alternatives to store-bought gift wrap: old maps, children's art, old calendar pages, posters, cloth napkins, scarves, fabric and, of course, the colourful pages of the newspaper. Mapwrap is made from surplus New York City subway maps (www.forestsaver.com).

Or you can make the wrapping part of the gift—for example, wrap a kitchen gift in an apron or tea towel or hide a book inside a magazine wrapped with raffia ribbon or twine. The more creative your choice, the more they *will* remember the wrapping.

Gift bags are an improvement over paper, since they are usually reused. But they are still often made using virgin paper that's bleached and dyed with harsh chemicals that wind up in the waste stream. Look for gift bags made from natural fibres, fabric or recycled content. You'll find gift bags made from 100 percent post-consumer recycled plastic at Gaiam (www.gaiam.com).

> GREENER GIFT TAGS My mother always hated spending money on those little gift tags that get thrown out in two seconds, so she taught us to cut cards out of wrapping scraps. My sister-in-law uses a decorative rubber stamp to jazz up a plain piece of scrap paper. And for the gift (tag) that keeps on giving, Bloomin' tags grow into wildflowers or blue spruce trees when planted in the ground (www.bloomin.com).

[26]
How to **Grow a Garden**

Whenever I'm wondering what it's going to take for people around the world to join forces toward a more sustainable way of living, I think about the Victory Gardens of World War II. Across Canada, England and the United States, citizens planted food gardens as a way to help lower the demand on public food supply during the wartime shortage. People who hadn't a clue about how to grow a potato planted all manner of crops in plots of whatever size they had available—a tiny front yard, a section of municipal land, a corner of a schoolyard.

What interests me about the Victory Gardens is the collective effort, harnessed by a sense of duty and responsibility to help in a time of crisis: the best of each for the good of all, as they say.

Do you think we still have it in us to rise together in a time of crisis, to each make our own small sacrifices to move history forward into a calmer, safer and healthier time?

I hope so.

In these global times there is no shortage of food in the Western larder, so you don't need to grow food to offset rationing. But the garden is your own tiny piece of Mother Earth—a small corner where your part of the collective revolution can begin. Your garden is also your respite from the rest of the world, a play space for your little people, an extension of your home when the Canadian seasons allow it. When your garden grows green for life, it is a relaxing oasis that can improve your health, not harm it. A garden that looks lovely thanks to chemical pesticides and synthetic fertilizers is a garden you don't want to set foot in.

THE SCARE:

A 1995 study in the *American Journal of Public Health* reported that children who live in homes where chemical pesticides and insecticides are used are four times more likely to develop cancer than those whose homes and gardens are pesticide free.

Breast cancer rates in North America have been rising since the 1940s—coinciding with the widespread introduction of chemical pesticides. The Sierra Club of Canada cautions against using pesticides as they contain organochlorines, which mimic estrogen and have been linked to breast cancer.

You may fall into the "but I like my gorgeous flower beds and I need those pesticides to keep them looking good!" category of gardener. Or, you may be on the other end of the green thumb spectrum, wondering how you could possibly learn enough or muster the time and effort to make any kind of garden grow, never mind one that is green for life.

Fear not. In whichever camp you find yourself, we have solutions: elegant, easy and manageable solutions to make your garden as healthy as it is gorgeous.

#1 Compost

If there were a competition for the most elegant and efficient green for life tip, composting would win, hands down. I know, smelly rotting orange peels and coffee grounds may not seem elegant at first glance, but hear me out.

The simple "from the earth, back to the earth" principle of biology makes composting an environmental one-two punch.

First of all, composting saves you having to schlep as much garbage to the curb each week: throwing food scraps into the compost bin instantly reduces household waste by as much as 40 percent. The more you compost, the less you send to landfill.

But wait, it gets better. *After* you've spared them from the landfill, those food scraps turn into "gardener's gold"—compost is an absolute boon to your garden. Leave those food scraps sitting in the hot sun in a covered container and watch what Mother Nature does for you: the earthy black stuff you pull out of the bottom of that bin in a few months is just about the best natural fertilizer you could ever want to put on your plants. Compost helps retain the moisture in the soil, nourishes and strengthens plants so they are more resistant to pests, and cuts down on weed growth—weeds prefer unhealthy soil.

Remember, throwing most of your food waste (see the box below for compost dos and don'ts) into a compost bin will (a) save you the heavy lifting on garbage day, (b) save you having to weed your garden as much, (c) save you money since you won't need synthetic fertilizers and (d) make you feel like an earth-saving green for life champion.

What are you waiting for? If the smell of compost turns you off, you just need a better container. Check out Lee Valley Tools (www.leevalley.com) for bins with charcoal filters in the lid; or for a more stylish fixture for your kitchen countertop, try their stainless steel canisters. I love mine: it never, ever smells, and it's big enough that we have to empty it only every couple of days.

Another way for you squeamish types to avoid the yicky factor is to use biodegradable compost bags—line your kitchen scrap bin with one and you won't have much cleaning to do. Check out www.ecoproducts.com for more information on "bio bags."

As for the outdoor bin, just make sure it's big and has access at the bottom, so you don't have to pick through soggy banana peels and flower clippings to get the good stuff out from underneath. Locate your bin in a sunny spot—the heat will speed the rate of decomposition. Note to urban homeowners: our city property is home to an extended multigenerational family of raccoons, and they *never* get into our compost. A secure lid is all you need to keep those nimble claws away.

You can find a composting bin to suit pretty much every residential scenario—rotating ones for those with little sun exposure, homemade chicken-wire rigs for those with a bigger piece of real estate, even worm compost (vermicompost) for apartment and condo dwellers. For all the information you could ever need or want about composting, check out the Composting Council of Canada at www.compost.org.

Looking to fertilize your garden naturally, but there's no compost in your bin? You can buy bags of premade

---

WHAT GOES IN THE COMPOST? DO put in: fruit and vegetables, grains, egg shells, baked goods, dryer lint, coffee grounds, tea bags, cardboard, animal hair/fur, nail clippings, droppings/litter from small animals, shredded newspaper, paper towels, faded flowers, sawdust, wood ashes, perennial weeds, grass clippings, non-plastic string **DON'T put in:** dairy products, meat, fish, bones, oils and fats, vacuum cleaner dust, disposable diapers, dog or cat droppings, plastic, chemicals, fabrics, large pieces of wood, diseased plants compost; other natural options are rock mineral, bone meal and blood meal. All these options serve as food for the soil's natural organisms, whereas chemical fertilizers actually destroy them.

#2 Water

Environment Canada reports that Canadians are among the highest water users in the world, second only to the United States. We have been criticized repeatedly by the Organisation for Economic Co-operation and Development (OECD) for our excessive use of water—65 percent above their international average. And our consumption tends to double in the summer, no doubt thanks in part to the advent of gardening season. We're so excited to see something growing after a long bleak winter that we water it like mad to make sure it sticks around.

But excessive watering is as bad for your plants as it is for our planet. Water your garden once a week *maximum*, for a longer time each watering. Light daily watering teaches the roots of grasses and plants to grow toward the surface, where they are vulnerable to heat. Watering during the heat of the day means most of that water will evaporate in the sun, and burn the plants in the meantime. Water in the early morning whenever possible; otherwise, water in the evening.

The best way to water plants is to use a hose with an adjustable nozzle—you can get the water directly on those thirsty roots. Trigger nozzles are invaluable so you don't waste water running back and forth to the tap to turn the hose on and off. You can make your life so much easier by grouping plants with similar water needs together.

If you're using a sprinkler on grass, try the good old-fashioned Frisbee trick: set an upside-down Frisbee on the area where you'll be watering—when the Frisbee is full, you're done. Grass needs about 2.5 centimetres (1 inch) of water once a week. So, you need to run the sprinkler only if it hasn't rained in the last week. Keep an eye on your watch to see how long it takes to fill the Frisbee. Then you can set a timer for your sprinkler for future watering.

Rainwater is perfect for plants: it's soft water, untreated with chlorine and fluoride, and at nature's perfect temperature. In a heavy rainstorm, every downspout on your house channels more than 40 litres of water into the storm sewer system *every minute*, which seems like such a waste of plant-perfect water. (On top of the waste, all that extra water overflows the sewer system catchment, so a lot of water ends up missing the treatment process altogether, discharging all manner of pollutants directly into nearby lakes and rivers.)

Well, if you can make hay while the sun shines, why not make plant water while it rains? To make the most of the free water supply, have your downspouts disconnected. Many municipalities provide the disconnection service for free, in the interest of taking the pressure off the storm sewer system. If you run your spouts directly into your garden beds, nature does even more of the watering for you. Otherwise, you can redirect the downspouts into a rainbarrel, which you can empty onto your garden once a week. Cover it with superfine mesh or a lid during dry spells, so it doesn't become a breeding ground for mosquitoes. How's that for a nice closed-loop watering system? Beats standing on the lawn in your bathrobe with a hose.

> **SPRINKLER 101** Run your sprinkler once a week at most, only if it hasn't rained all week, in the early morning or early evening, until an upside-down Frisbee on the lawn is full, or with a sprinkler timer or your watch set.

#3 Mulch

Mulch is a champion of the garden, especially for those of us who don't like to spend our entire weekend labouring on the lawn. Mulch is really just protective material put on the earth around your plants. It helps retain moisture, stops weed growth and moderates soil temperatures—protecting the soil and plants from the elements. As organic mulch breaks down over time, it adds nutrients to the soil. You often see plants surrounded by wood chips or bark bits—that's mulch. But there are loads of materials you can use to mulch.

Perhaps the cheapest and easiest mulch is leaf mould. Now I know that sounds scary and yucky, but it's really just composted leaves. When you're doing your fall cleanup, fill a green garbage bag with leaves and add a shovelful of dirt. Leave it over the winter, and presto! Leaf mould. Sprinkle it around new plantings in the spring to give them a boost of nutrients. Toronto Public Health says fresh fallen leaves can be left in a seven-centimetre (three-inch) layer on garden beds over the winter for a protective mulch that's cheap at twice the price.

HOW TO TACKLE THOSE DANDELIONS ONCE AND FOR ALL Since we're no longer exposing ourselves and our neighbours to toxic chemicals by using pesticides, here's a better way to get rid of those unwanted yellow menaces.

Cut off their heads. (Doesn't that feel therapeutic?) Now they can no longer reproduce, so eventually they will stop growing. Pull out the roots of the ones that are left—without weeding, the problem will grow. Remember, weeds like poor soil, so read about compost in #1, above.

After all your hard work, relax with a warm pot of dandelion tea.

You can also buy bagged materials for mulching—pine bark, wood chips and shredded bark or "forest mulch." A commercial product called SoilSponge, made mostly from coconut fibre, absorbs water then releases it as soil dries out. Proponents say it adds an extra week to your time between waterings, and saves flower beds and potted plants when you are on vacation or just forget to water.

For more detailed information about mulch, including a table of common mulching materials and their nutrient properties, check out the no-till gardening article at www.eartheasy.com.

#4 Xeriscaping

This is a complex word that is easy to master. Xeriscape was coined by combining the Greek word *xeros*, which means dry, with "landscape." It means landscaping in a way that doesn't require extra irrigation, which makes it a brilliant strategy for the lazy gardeners among us.

How do you like the sounds of watering as little as once a month? Imagine, that's basically five times a summer! Now that's my kind of gardener's discipline.

All you have to do is plant native and drought-resistant plants, apply lots of mulch, then sit back and enjoy the beauty of your hassle-free garden.

In general, drought-resistant plants will have broad roots and small leaves, sometimes with a waxy coating on the leaves. Look in your area for municipal water-saving initiatives that may include information on xeriscaping. The city of Regina gets such little moisture in the summer, they offer xeriscaping workshops. For lists of drought-resistant plants that grow well in your area, check out www.eartheasy.com.

Native plants

If it comes from here, it was meant to be here, and it will do well here. It's a fairly basic principle that we have kind of lost touch with in the global village these days. The same way we buy Bartlett pears from Argentina in January, we plant Japanese maples and English roses in our gardens, and then we wonder why it takes so much water and fertilizer to make them grow.

Most of the soil in Canada is quite alkaline, on average; many of those fancy imported plants need acidity to do well. That's why you have to work so hard to curry their favour and coax a bloom out of them.

Planting native plants takes a lot of the stress out of your gardening—plants that are indigenous to your local soil and climate will automatically fare better. As a bonus, native plants are popular with the locals: they attract more butterflies, birds and native bugs like ladybugs, which not only make your garden feel like a natural oasis, but often are natural predators for garden pests like slugs and aphids.

For a list of plants that are native to your area, check out the Canadian Wildlife Federation's website at www.wildaboutgardening.org.

 ## Grass 101

When you're seeding your lawn, look for the hardiest grass possible. Kentucky bluegrass is a popular-selling grass seed in Canada, but, as its name would suggest, it is hardly indigenous. As a result it is not very hardy and demands moist roots. No wonder Canada's water consumption doubles in the summer—we're trying to trick our lawns into thinking they're below the Mason–Dixon Line.

Fescues and ryegrasses are less thirsty types of grass. Eco-Lawn grass seed grows in sun or shade with little to no water, so it's the hot new environmental choice for grass. Not genetically modified, it has naturally long roots to suit our northern climate, and it grows so slowly you hardly ever have to cut it! Check it out for yourself at www.wildflowerfarms.com.

"Mow high" is the mantra for green for life grass cutting—but don't go using narcotics while operating a power mower and blaming me for what happens. First of all, you want to trade in that gas mower—according to Environment Canada, Canadians use 150 million litres of gasoline every year to run power lawn mowers; the California Environmental Protection Agency says just one gas mower emits the same amount of smog-causing emissions each hour as 40 new cars over the same time. Take your gas guzzler to the Home Depot for a rebate on a push mower or at least an electric one—and make it snappy.

Anyway, back to the narcotics. "Mow high" refers to the length of blade you leave when you mow. Researchers at the University of Guelph have established seven centimetres (three inches) as the ideal length for grass to be cut to—it's long enough to retain extra moisture, plus the added height creates shade, which prevents weed growth. Keep your mower blades sharp so you cut the grass rather than rip it.

Now, after a tough afternoon of pushing a lawn mower across your grass, do you really feel like raking all those clippings up, bagging them and dragging them to the curb for pickup? Okay, then don't. Use your new-found environmentalism as your justification for leaving the darn things right where they are. Toronto Public Health says 18 percent of garbage in North America is grass clippings. The crazy part is, those young, short grass ends decompose quickly; give off nitrogen and potassium and phosphorous, which are natural fertilizers; and help your lawn retain moisture. Your work here is done.

But if it's a work-free lawn you're after, you're going to want to reconsider that grass altogether. I mean, it is basically green cement. Reduce the amount of grass space (and therefore your mowing job) by extending your flower beds. Or if you still need the open space to run around, replace it with some other ground cover. We've used clover, a fabulous and hardy alternative to grass, in our backyard. And my eldest son is destined for a life of good luck after finding a whole bunch of four-leaf clovers. For more alternative ground cover ideas, check out www.thegardenhelper.com/groundcover.html.

 ## #7 Pesticides

Several municipalities in Canada have officially banned pesticides for commercial and residential use, even though they are still sold in some stores.

Most of the chemicals used in pesticides were approved for use in the 1950s *and have not been regulated since*. If you plot on a graph the increase in use of pesticides since their advent after World War II, and then plot the rise in the rates of cancers, allergies and learning disabilities, you will note a chilling parallel. According to a

> GARDEN PARTY TRICK Heels or cleats on the lawn? Sure! Dance the night away in your spikes to aerate the grass, creating passages that allow air, water and nutrients to reach the roots. A more traditional, but maybe less fun approach, is to buy aerating shoes, available through companies like Lee Valley Tools (www.leevalley.com). You can also rent an aerating roller from your local garden store. Do it in June or September, then follow with compost.

1995 report in the *American Journal of Public Health*, children in homes where chemical weed and insect killers were used are four times more likely to develop cancer. The Sierra Club of Canada claims a clear link between pesticide use and breast cancer. And for the same reason that they wipe out the pests on your plants, pesticides are also toxic to birds, beneficial insects and ultimately fish when they run off lawns and gardens into the water system.

Healthier plants, treated to the natural nutrients of compost and organic mulch, will be more able to resist pests naturally. For a little added help, don't attack nature with pesticides; instead, put nature to work for you. Ladybugs are brilliant natural pest control. Buglady Consulting (www.bugladyconsulting.com) provides links to suppliers of beneficial insects such as ladybugs. Just let them loose in your garden like a bunch of little Clint Eastwoods. Go ahead, aphid, make my day.

Remineralizing the soil in the spring and then again in the fall is another way to boost its nutrient content enough so that you'll never need to use pesticides or fertilizers. Ask at your local garden store about rock or gravel dust and read the primer at www.remineralize.org.

BEATING BACKYARD BUGS If you're spritzing DEET, you should know that it is a neurotoxin; if you're using citronella repellents on the skin, you should know that Health Canada has phased them out over the last few years pending further regulatory safety tests. Essential oils mixed with an unscented oil base have been proven effective against bugs; see Chapter 21, "How to Raise Healthy Kids," for more ideas about natural repellents. The Sierra Club website has super-easy all-natural spray recipes for repellents too (www.sierraclub.ca). Also try installing a bat house to attract the mosquito's natural predator.

The Sierra Club of Canada offers a fabulous selection of natural pest control sprays you can whip up in two seconds—use things as innocuous as garlic, flour and vegetable oil to keep your garden free of nasty predators *and* nasty chemicals. Search "pest control" at www.sierraclub.ca for a handful of easy recipes.

 ## No-till gardening

New research out of Ohio State University suggests that when we dig or till the soil before planting or to reduce weeds, most of the soil's carbon is released into the atmosphere in the form of carbon dioxide. No-till gardening is one way to help reduce these carbon emissions. It simply involves adding layers of soil and compost on top of what's already there—which is why it is also called lasagna gardening. It even works to help eliminate weeds. Smother them with additional layers of compost and topsoil—kill them with kindness, as it were.

Search "no-till gardening" at www.eartheasy.com for a full primer on how to make your flower beds into an outdoor lasagna.

 ## The barbecue

It's a staple of many Canadian backyards in the summer. And while a marinated tofu-kebab or a burger just doesn't taste as good any other way, barbecuing contributes lung-harming particles to the air in your yard and contributes to ground-level ozone—affectionately known as smog.

So what is a hungry green for lifer to do on a summer's night during barbecue season? That depends on what kind of grill you've got. If you're still using charcoal briquettes, they've got to go. I know it's the traditional method of choice for barbecuing, but charcoal also gives off more carbon monoxide, particulate matter and soot than other methods, according to the Sierra Club. Briquettes are made from the scraps and sawdust from lumber mills with a handful of additives to bind it all together.

If you can't let go of the smoky flavour, at least switch to lump charcoal, which is unprocessed and comes straight from the tree. The Sierra Club also recommends you look for charcoal that is certified by the Rainforest Alliance's SmartWood program. Check out www.wickedgoodcharcoal.com for 100 percent natural and unprocessed lump charcoal.

The best barbecue bet is to cook with a propane burner or an electric grill—you can count that kind of grill cooking as ozone free. Or if you want to do your outdoor cooking the way Ed Begley Jr., does, how about a solar oven? It'll have about the same cooking season as a barbecue. Just face it to the south and let nature make dinner!

[27]
How to **Run an Office**

Whether you're the big boss of the home office or a cog in the machine of a corporate empire, you can still make your green for life voice heard. And it *must* be heard—office buildings are among the most environmentally unfriendly places around.

So where do you start? How do you shift the corporate culture? Where else but the bottom line. It's what every boss lives and dies by. Interestingly, more and more companies are operating by what's called the triple bottom line: considering the financial, social and environmental impacts of their business practices—and thriving for it.

Office greening saves money, which is always popular. And if you're the one who nudges the office culture down a greener path to savings? Well, we know who's getting the next promotion, don't we?

#1 Start with how you get to work

Before you start greening your office team, start with yourself. Are you one of the 64 percent of Canadians who drive to work every day in a single passenger car? Wow, all that money spent on gas, parking and insurance is eating up a decent portion of your paycheque. And all that driving is certainly contributing to smog buildup and to Canada's greenhouse gas emissions—13 percent comes from personal transportation. Explore other options: take public transit, even if only part of the time. Place a notice on the company bulletin board or through interoffice email for carpooling. Check out www.vivacommute.com to find people who do a similar commute in your area.

 ## Power down lights and computers

How many times do you shut down your computer when you head off on your lunch break? I once hosted a show about saving energy around the home and interviewed a family who had never turned off their computer! Sounds extreme, but it's not that unusual in our culture—we tend to leave office appliances on so they are ready for us on command. The U.S. Department of Energy recommends turning off your computer monitor if you'll be gone for more than 20 minutes, and shutting down the whole computer if you will be away from your desk for any more than two hours. Remember that a screen saver does not save energy—it may actually use more!

What kind of computer are you labouring at? Laptop computers use 50 percent less energy than desktops; whatever model you have, make sure you set the sleep mode to kick in after five minutes of inactivity.

If you're working on a desktop computer with an old cathode ray tube (CRT) monitor, see if you can get it replaced with a liquid crystal display (LCD) screen. Not only does it look sleeker and take up less space, but it uses up to 75 percent less energy than a CRT monitor of equal size.

And as with all appliances, at home or at the office, look for the Energy Star logo when you buy a new one, to ensure you'll be using the least amount of energy.

Even after they are switched off, electronic appliances are often drawing "phantom power" in standby mode, ready to be fired up on a moment's notice. So even when they're off, they're not off, if you follow me. Connect all your machinery to a power bar with the switch in easy reach, then flick *that* off. (Remember this at home too for TVs, VCRs, DVD players and other home entertainment appliances that are costing you in electricity when they're not fully off.)

After you've turned off your computer, be sure to turn off the lights as well. Make it the new office habit to turn off lights when you leave the boardroom or the bathroom, or look into occupancy sensors, which take on that responsibility for you. If that's not an option, a simple reminder note on the light switch is remarkably effective. Roughly 25 percent of a building's energy costs are for lighting—so leaving them on overnight makes absolutely no financial sense. And if your office is in a glass office tower, lights left on at night could actually be killing birds. The Fatal Light Awareness Program (FLAP) estimates that 100 million birds die in North America every year in collisions with buildings, drawn to the artificial light source from office lights left on overnight.

You probably already have a few compact fluorescent (CFL) light bulbs at home, but they make even more sense in offices, where lights are left on for so long. Because CFLs use a fraction of the energy of incandescent bulbs and they last five to eight times longer, they pay for themselves in no time.

Remember that even if your office is taking extra steps to offset its energy consumption with either green

GET CHEEKY TO SAVE ENERGY **Tell your co-workers to flick off! This Canadian action campaign is full of great tips and tools for conserving energy, as well as inspiring examples of corporate leadership on sustainability. Check out www.flickoff.org—you can even find a nifty reminder sticker for those light switches.**

electricity through companies such as Bullfrog Power (www.bullfrogpower.com) or carbon offsets, reducing your consumption will always be the first and most significant step you should take. (See Chapter 28, "How to Plan a Holiday," for more of the cold hard truth about carbon offsets.)

 ## #3 Use less paper

Do you really need to print that memo, or can it just be sent as an email? Would a projection screen in the meeting room eliminate the need for all those handouts? The amount of paper that offices go through in a day is staggering. According to Environment Canada, it takes 19 full-grown trees (that's a total of some 570 years of growth) just to make one ton of virgin office paper. And the chlorine bleach used to make printer paper so crispy white produces persistent dioxin, a human carcinogen.

Not all papers are created equal: look for chlorine-free paper that is post-consumer recycled (PCR)—that means it's made from paper products that have already been used, so if it contains 100 percent PCR content no new trees were cut down to produce it. The Forest Stewardship Council (FSC) certifies forests that are being sustainably managed. More companies are switching to Forest Stewardship Council (FSC)–certified paper for their printing jobs—in October 2007, no lesser work than the Bible was printed on FSC-certified and recycled paper for the first time. Surely it's good enough for your annual report. Some forward-thinking businesses, including World Wildlife Fund Canada, now send out a virtual annual report—no paper required.

Print (only when necessary!) on both sides of the page—most new copiers are equipped with a "duplexing" feature that uses both sides of the paper.

For a catalogue of recycled "tree-free" paper and office products for all your business needs, check out www.greenlinepaper.com.

#4 Recycle

It's the most popular of the three Rs, but you'd be surprised how little it happens in the workplace, which is odd considering this is the place where the cost of removing waste is arguably highest. Since companies pay to have waste removed, management might be interested in having someone analyze your company's office waste to look for savings by recycling or composting.

As a first step, be sure everyone understands how to separate their waste properly. Put clearly marked paper-recycling bins beside the photocopier and the printer, and get individual ones for everyone to put next to the garbage pail at their desk.

If you are using non-recyclable paper, you can put it through the shredder and use the bits for packing material in the mail room.

Recycling is for more than just paper. Printers' ink cartridges should be returned to the manufacturer instead of thrown away. According to Office Depot, every toner cartridge that gets "remanufactured" keeps more than a kilogram of metal and plastic out of landfill and saves nearly two litres of oil.

#5 Overhaul the office kitchen

It's the one place in the office where you can feel like your old self and not a worker bee. You can grab a snack, pour some coffee, take a respite from the grind.

The office kitchen can be the best place to start your green revolution by posting green for life tips on the kitchen notice board, or chatting up some ideas with colleagues over a fair trade organic coffee. Once people notice how much better the fresh roasted organic coffee tastes, they'll start waking up to a greener approach! Ask everyone to bring in their own coffee mug so the company can stop paying for those disposable cups. Whether they're Styrofoam or coated cardboard cups, they're non-recyclable in most municipalities. According to the U.S. Environmental Protection Agency, the cup you used this morning will still be sitting in a landfill in 500 years, along with the other 25 billion Styrofoam cups thrown away every year.

For a full purge of wasteful products from the kitchen, lose those wooden or plastic stirsticks—a drawerful of stainless steel spoons will do the trick for a lot less money in the long run.

COFFEE WITH EXTRA ADJECTIVES After petroleum, coffee is the second most valuable commodity in the world—small wonder, considering it's pretty much a requirement for most of us to get out the door and into work every day. Whether you get your fix from the machine at home, the barista on the corner or the office coffeemaker, you should know that your daily habit has a massive impact that reaches far around the globe. Choose organic fair trade coffee, which is grown and processed without toxic chemicals and harvested in ways that protect the surrounding ecosystem. *Organic* beans also spare the workers from exposure to harmful pesticides; *fair trade* assures that they are paid a living wage for their back-breaking work. *Shade grown* is another adjective to add to your latte order. Whereas many plantations have cut down all the surrounding trees to make room for more coffee plants, beans grown in shade preserve habitat for wildlife.

#6 Avoid plastic water bottles

Some offices buy bottled water to serve at meetings or just to keep the staff happy and hydrated. This seems like awfully thoughtful corporate culture, but before you get feeling too warm and fuzzy over the gesture, consider the environmental cost. StatCan says that 30 percent of Canadians drink predominantly bottled water. The Pacific Institute reports that producing the plastic bottles requires 17 million barrels of oil, not including transportation; bottling the water produces more than 2.5 million tons of carbon dioxide. And it takes three litres of water to produce one litre of bottled water. What's worse, the Union of Concerned Scientists says that 90 percent of water bottles are not recycled, so they will live out the next zillion years in a landfill, breaking down ever so slowly long after you and I are gone.

And besides, in Canada, local water supplies are inspected every day, whereas bottled water facilities are inspected at three-year intervals. In 2004, 500,000 bottles of Coca-Cola's Dasani water were recalled in the British market because they were found to contain high levels of bromate, a cancer-causing chemical.

If you're buying brands like Coca-Cola's Dasani (or Pepsi's Aquafina), you should know that you're paying good money for filtered municipal tap water—in Canada, Dasani water is bottled in Brampton, Ontario, and in Calgary.

While the jumbo water dispenser—better known as the water cooler, or gossip central—is a refillable alternative to so many little bottles, it is not without its share of concerns. Global Industry Group research has found low levels of bisphenol A (BPA) from those big plastic water dispensers leaching into the water. The longer it sits there, the more it can leach.

BPA mimics the action of the human hormone estrogen, and it can stimulate prostate cancer cells, cause ovarian dysfunction and alter immune function; it has also been linked to breast cancer. A U.S. Centers for Disease Control and Prevention study found BPA in 95 percent of the adults sampled. For probably less than the monthly water service charges, your company could install a filter on the water intake pipe at the kitchen sink. Filtered municipal water, drunk from a glass, not a plastic cup or bottle, is your best bet for daily hydration.

Or for a more durable (and portable) vessel, get yourself a new stainless steel bottle. Check out www.kleankanteen.com, www.lifewithoutplastic.com or visit a Mountain Equipment Co-op store.

#7 Go for green office furniture

Is it your job that's giving you the headache, or is it the rugs? Sick building syndrome isn't just a paranoid theory of the whiny office hypochondriac—it's very real and increasingly common. The air quality in an office building gets "sick" from a combination of poor ventilation and chemical contamination. Poor ventilation obviously stems from windows that don't open and ducting systems that function improperly either from ineffective design or lack of maintenance. The chemical contamination comes from the synthetic carpeting found in virtually every office building. The carpet is usually made of petroleum-based fibres, and the nylon backing, foam padding and adhesives used to install it are all off-gassing a slew of volatile organic compounds (VOCs), including formaldehyde, toluene and xylene. Toxicology studies out of Anderson Laboratories in Massachusetts have shown that blowing warm air through some carpet samples into mice cages for a total of four hours over two days *can kill the mice*. Small wonder people keep pain relief in their desk drawer.

If new carpets are on the agenda, there are several carpet manufacturers that produce low-emission synthetic carpets. Direct management's attention to Interface, the largest—and greenest—commercial carpet manufacturer in the world. Interface carpets are designed with recyclability in mind, using materials that are renewable. Interface takes responsibility for the end-of-life for their products by removing worn out carpets and recycling them.

If you aren't likely to get new carpets anytime soon, make sure to get yourself outside several times a day for some fresh air.

#8 Stop electronic waste

Everybody loves a new computer. But in this age of planned obsolescence, the way we deal with our old computers, cell phones and other electronics has a huge impact on the earth. Though they're shiny and funky on the outside, many of our favourite gizmos are full of toxins such as mercury, cadmium and carcinogenic PCBs on their insides; wires are coated with polyvinyl chloride (PVC) plastic; many glass screens are made with lead.

DOING WELL BY DOING GOOD Ray Anderson is the kind of boss you want to have or aspire to be. The CEO of Interface decided in 1994 that he didn't want to be part of the problem anymore. He has committed to being totally sustainable by 2010—using reusable, renewable and recyclable fibres in the carpets the company manufactures. The cost of his green agenda? A savings of $120 million U.S., actually. Anderson has made Interface the largest and most successful commercial carpet manufacturer in the world. Tell that to your employers if they say the company can't afford to go green.

Environment Canada projects that by 2010, Canadian homes and businesses will produce more than 400,000 tons of e-waste. We don't want all that in our waste and water streams, so we ship it to China. Lower environmental standards and cheaper working conditions make countries like China, India and Kenya popular destinations for North America's electronic waste.

What a lot of people don't realize is that there's gold in those electronic devices: 1 ton of scrap from discarded computers contains more gold than can be produced from 17 tons of gold ore. In Europe, reclaiming and repurposing the parts from electronics is mandatory for manufacturers. In Canada, some pioneering companies, most notably Hewlett-Packard, are voluntarily closing the loop on their own manufacturing, reusing old materials in new products. HP Canada's Planet Partners return and recycling program makes it easy to return your printing equipment, computer hardware and rechargeable batteries to them. By salvaging valuable plastics and metals, and recycling what cannot be reused, HP's program has diverted millions of tons of e-waste from landfills. Check out www.hp.ca/recycle to order a bag or box to return your HP gear to them, free of charge.

For other computers that have reached the end of their life, be sure to recycle them through an organization such as the Electronic Recycling Association in

DON'T TOSS THOSE BATTERIES! Batteries must be disposed of in hazardous waste facilities, though most aren't, or they leach acids and other corrosives into the groundwater. For all your Dictaphones, recorders and labellers, be sure to invest in some rechargeable batteries. Check out the myriad options, including solar chargers, at www.greenbatteries.com.

the West (www.era.ca) or Recycle Comps in Quebec (www.recyclecomps.com). The Manitoba government offers electronic recycling as well (www.gov.mb.ca).

#9 Replace your answering machine

Smaller offices that still have a good old-fashioned answering machine, listen up. You may not be paying for a call-answering service, but you are paying for electricity to keep that machine plugged in 24 hours a day. And since most of our electricity comes from oil- or coal-fired plants, it creates a whole lot of air pollution and greenhouse gases. The U.S. Energy Information Administration says that if every answering machine on the continent were replaced with voice mail, the reduction in air pollution would be the same as taking 250,000 cars off the road each year. Get the message?

How to **Plan a Holiday**

If you haven't spent all your money on organic food and solar panels, you may be able to take a vacation. Oh, the thrill of closing your desk drawer for the last time before getting out of town, or waving goodbye to those hollering children as you pull out of the drive for a well-deserved getaway. Holidays have a way of putting all the stress and struggle of our daily routines into perspective and making every challenge seem more manageable.

But while you don't have to recycle the printer cartridges or empty the kitchen compost bin while you're on vacation, you'll still want to take a moment to consider the impact of your travel on the earth. You may be on holiday, but your footprint travels with you.

For help in figuring out how to make a green for life getaway, read on. But remember that some of the most important things you can do for the earth while you're travelling happen before you even step out the door.

It's so easy to get caught up in the excitement and stress about getting where you're going that you may forget to consider what you're leaving behind. As you tear out the door and jump into the taxi, don't just double-check that you've remembered your passport—double-check that you've vacation-proofed your house.

Even if you're just skipping town for the weekend, turn down the heat or air conditioning—you don't want to pay for heating or cooling when no one is at home! A programmable thermostat allows you to set the system to turn back on just before you return, so you can come home to a comfortable house.

Unplug or switch off everything but your fridge. Even when they're not in use, appliances are drawing "phantom power"—for example, to keep a television in standby mode or run the clock on a microwave or video recorder. Plugging all your home entertainment appliances into a power bar makes it easy to power them all down with the flip of a switch. To avoid wasting (and paying for) electricity, do a little flick-off walk through your house just before you leave—be sure to include the hot water heater, which should be turned way down or put on a vacation setting.

Did the safety proofers tell you to leave lights on when you're out of town so your house isn't an obvious target for burgling? Better yet, put some lights on timers. These simple devices, sold at any hardware store, turn your lights on and off automatically, making the house look even more lived in and saving on your electricity bill.

Put a hold on newspaper delivery. Cancelling your newspaper service while you're away saves paper, which saves trees, which saves the earth.

Draw the shades over your windows to keep the heat in during winter and out during summer. That way your furnace or air conditioner will have less work to do when you return.

Now your house is ready to be energy efficient in your absence. The next step for the green for life traveller is to consider five important questions.

 ## Where should you go?

How well do you know your own backyard? I mean, how much have you explored your home province, or even the rest of Canada? Because in the "new morality," as world-renowned environmental journalist George Monbiot calls it, travelling to your cousin's wedding halfway around the world is actually a bad thing, because of the carbon emissions it takes to get you there. If you're going that far for pure pleasure, I think he'd call you, as my four-year-old would say, a super-duper bad guy.

Travel close to home. Sounds like an oxymoron, but since emissions from airplanes make up roughly 10 percent of the world's greenhouse gas emissions it's time to start thinking more creatively about where we go and how we get there. Explore travel options closer to where you live, starting with websites like www.trailcanada.com and www.canadiantravelguide.net.

 ## #2 How should you get there?

Virgin Fuels, a subsidiary of Richard Branson's airline company, is scrambling to come up with biofuel for jet planes. The rock 'n' roll CEO told me in an interview that Virgin is hoping to fly a jet on biofuel before 2010. But it will be a long time before technology can save us, so in the interim we have to make a conscious effort to fly less.

Airplane emissions are among the most egregious offenders. Because they take place so high in the sky, spewing those greenhouse gases right next to the atmosphere, they're even more damaging than ground-level emissions.

So how do you get around if you're stuck on the ground? Driving a car, especially a single-passenger vehicle, is certainly not a solution, unless of course you're carpooling in a new hybrid.

The best way to travel while being gentler on the atmosphere is to go by train. Good old-fashioned adventure on the rails has been fodder for countless films and children's stories—now it's the eco-chic travel mode of choice.

Mark Smith must have been one of those train set addicts as a boy, because he grew up to become the Man in Seat Sixty-One, creator of an award-winning site for responsible tourism, www.seat61.com. It's full of routes and itineraries for flight-free travel to and from the UK, where the site is based, but also within other countries, including Canada and the United States. For more ideas on getting around North America by train, check out www.usa-by-rail.com.

If you're feeling sporty, try dusting off your old pedals. Travelling by bicycle is the best way to see the sights up close and at your own pace, and to connect more intimately with the people and places you visit. Join Canada's national cycling network and become part of the Tour du Canada (www.tourducanada.com), the longest annual bike ride in the world that lets you get to know your home and native land in a whole new way. Several travel companies have chosen two wheels over four, from the rugged excursion for outdoor enthusiasts with organizations like the Adventure Cycling Association (www.adventurecycling.org) to a luxury holiday with Butterfield & Robinson, a company with a strong environmental commitment (www.butterfield.com). Not only do they offset all their air travel with carbon credits,

> **HOLIDAY IN A HYBRID** If you're renting a car to get around, make it a hybrid. More and more car rental companies are adding hybrids to their fleets, including Discount in Ontario and ViaRoute in Quebec. Hertz has recently added a few thousand hybrids to 50 airport locations across the United States. Ask for a hybrid at Enterprise rentals—they are introducing them into more markets every month. It's a great opportunity to test drive a hybrid if you're thinking of buying one back home.

they print their trip catalogue on Forest Stewardship Council (FSC)–certified paper, serve organic fair trade coffee and power their business with alternative energy. Their decades-old relationships with hotels around the world are also helping B&R influence the greening of the hotel industry. For DIY adventure ideas, check out www.bikeontours.on.ca and www.cyclecanada.com, or pick up a copy of *Canadian Bicycle Tours* by Jerry Dennis.

If you've just *got* to go and flying is the *only* way to get there, consider buying carbon credits to offset the climate-changing impact of your travel. Buying carbon credits is like making a peace offering to the global warming gods—you put 15 tons of carbon into the atmosphere flying to your brother's wedding in Australia, so you pay for 15 tons of credit to offset that action. You can calculate your carbon impact through the Vancouver company Green My Flight (www.greenmyflight.com), but be sure to do your research before you decide whom to buy offsets from. Depending on which company you support,

---

CLEARING THE AIR ABOUT CARBON CREDITS

"Carbon offsets" is becoming a bit of a buzz phrase these days. But the important thing to remember is that we cannot buy our way out of global warming. Carbon offsets are not your free pass to emit greenhouse gasses carelessly. Once you've reduced your use of fossil fuels and supported more efficient technology, *then* you can buy some carbon credits to help close the gap, to offset emissions you cannot completely erase. Turn off lights first, switch to compact fluorescent bulbs, then invest in green powering your company or your home.

So if you normally take ten flights a year, your first step is to cut that back to three. Those you can offset with carbon credits.

you'll either pay for trees to be planted or cleaner energy to be produced. If you're paying to plant trees as your offset, remember that it will take several decades for those trees to absorb the greenhouse gas that your flight produces right now—and even that is guaranteed only if the trees reach maturity and don't die off in a drought or get cut down. Will the company you bought the offsets from be around for 30 years to monitor the trees' growth? Will they replant them if they die before reaching maturity? A safer bet is to buy credits from an organization that invests in alternative energy. Climate Friendly in Australia (www.climatefriendly.com) and Clean Air Pass in Canada (www.cleanairpass.com) are both reputable outfits—offsetting with them means supporting the transition to clean energy and investing in technologies that will be part of the solution. You'll be in good company. David Suzuki offset his cross-Canada bus tour in 2007, and Coldplay and Pearl Jam have both released carbon-neutral albums.

 ### #3 What should you do there?

Put your money where your values are and visit parks and nature reserves wherever you travel. Your entry fee will certainly support those existing protected areas, and it may also lead to the protection of additional sections of nature.

You may feel like a virtuous camper or traveller who never litters and always hikes responsibly, but even though you may be alone on the beach or trail, more folks will follow in your wake. Over time, travellers have an impact on any region. Be sure that when you are in nature, you follow the golden rule: take nothing but photographs, leave nothing but footprints.

My mother used to return from beach holidays with boxes of rocks and shells for me to play with. And while I marvel at her cost-savings and ingenuity—teaching a child to be more excited about nature than a toy from the airport!—it really isn't a habit we should continue. Don't remove rocks, shells, corals, dried fish, etc. from their natural environment. Every piece of nature is a vital part of an ecosystem. Take a digital photograph instead. It will take up less space in your house.

There are those for whom no holiday would be complete without some time on the golf course. But did you know that golf courses are notorious eco-villains?

Countless pesticides are sprayed on most golf courses, about 4.5 kilograms of nitrogen fertilizer are used per 100 square metres of grass, and they are irrigated with enormous amounts of water—a single course can require up to 375 million litres of water per year. So, try to support more progressive courses that recycle water. Ask golf course managers to go green on the greens and tell them you'd like to play the game as it originated in Scotland, over wild grasses and natural landscapes. In the meantime, be sure to wash your hands when you've finished playing. You can be sure they're covered in pesticide residue.

If you're a boater, rather than a golfer, be aware that the amount of fuel and oil pollution entering North America's waterways from recreational boating is roughly one billion litres. That's more than 15 times the amount of the *Exxon Valdez* oil spill—every year.

NO BODY PARTS IN YOUR LUGGAGE There's nothing like a souvenir to bring home a little piece of your holiday. But you don't want your holiday memories stained with death and destruction. Be sure you're not unwittingly supporting illegal activity. Never buy trinkets made from animal parts such as ivory, tortoise shell, coral or animal hides. Don't support the industry of exploiting wildlife.

If you have a power boat, consider putting a four-stroke engine on it. If your motor is more than a few years old, it's probably a two-stroke, which means nearly 50 percent of the fuel passing through its combustion chamber remains unburned and goes directly into the water. Not a model of efficiency.

A four-stroke engine burns 40 to 80 percent less fuel, doesn't require oil, reduces hydrocarbon emissions by up to 90 percent, and is a lot quieter too. It will pay for itself quickly in gas savings.

Be sure to fill your tank onshore and not over water, to avoid spilling fuel directly into the waterway. Use non-toxic cleaners to keep your darling vessel squeaky clean. (For more on natural cleaners and non-toxic recipes, see Chapter 3, "How to Clean the Kitchen," and Chapter 4, "How to Remove Stains.")

#4 Where should you stay?

Make sure you stay at a hotel that is making some demonstrable commitment to the environment. According to the Washington, D.C., research institute Resources for the Future, the average hotel room uses

---

WATER PIGS It's not the incessant buzz of those whiny little motors that gets me. It's not the fact that the pitch of the motor is just the right frequency to interrupt any afternoon nap. It's the pollution of Jet Skis and personal watercraft that really kills me—and kills fish. Jet Ski engines exhaust nitrogen oxides, carbon monoxides and cancer-causing hydrocarbons. The California Air Resources Board says that a day of jet skiing releases as many air pollutants as driving a car 223,000 kilometres. Look for another way to have fun—and let the canoeists get back to their naps.

upwards of 150 gallons (560 litres) of water per day. Many hotels have a little sign in the bathroom offering you the chance to save water by using your sheets and towels for more than one night.

If the hotel doesn't offer this water-saving program, suggest that they do. Make a specific request to the hotel manager that they not replace the sheets, towels and soaps during your stay.

In most new hotels in Europe, your room key also activates the power, so you can't leave the room without deactivating it. Otherwise, you'll have to remember that one yourself—turn off the lights, radio and television when you leave the room.

Before you check in to your hotel, ask if they Check Out for Nature. Participating hotels in this program donate the equivalent of one euro to World Wildlife Fund for every guest that checks out. To learn more about how to choose your holiday hotel wisely, search hotels at www.panda.org. For a listing of Canadian and U.S. hotels that are going green, check out www.terrachoice.com and look for the ones with the most "Green Leafs." The Green Hotels Association offers criteria for green hotel practices, as well as tips for greening your own choices while you're away (www.greenhotels.com).

#5 What should you bring?

It's the golden rule of packing: estimate the bare minimum of what you think you'll need on the trip, then cut it in half. You don't need to be an environmentalist, just a smart traveller to know that. But if you're looking for another reason to reduce your travel essentials, remember that extra weight means extra fuel to transport it.

Whenever possible, take carry-on luggage only. Everyone has a story of lost luggage to scare you off the checked baggage belt, but remember too that the baggage carousel runs on electricity, and it runs longer the more bags are on it. Save the energy by packing light and just bringing carry-on.

Pack your own toiletries. Hotel shampoos and lotions use millions of tiny plastic bottles that create a massive amount of waste and not all hotels have proper recycling programs. Also, those products are usually heavily scented and seldom contain natural ingredients, so you'll be dousing yourself in a chemical bath if you're using hotel suds. Pack a couple of small plastic bags so you can bring home your unused soap, and bring your laundry home where you can wash it yourself more efficiently (in cold water with your biodegradable soaps! See Chapter 5, "How to Do Laundry," for more). Travelling with kids? Bring an LED nightlight so you don't have to leave the bathroom light on all night. Wind-up LED flashlights are the only way to go for a camping holiday, or any other trip that might require a portable light source. Powered by a crank that you turn on the side of the handle, they

THE EVOLUTION OF GUIDEBOOKS AND MAPS

When I was a student backpacker, in the misty Precambrian days before the Internet, I remember carrying my bright orange and well-thumbed copy of *Let's Go Europe* wherever I went—all 684 pages of it. Now, of course, you can search virtually all your travel info online and print only what you absolutely need.

The same goes for maps, which are hard to recycle because of all the coloured ink used on the paper. Use online maps, printing when you need to, on paper that you can easily recycle. Many rental cars (all of those in Europe, in fact) now have built-in GPS navigation systems, so you may not need a printed map at all. Except you can't throw the GPS out the window when you're lost and mad at your husband.

never run out of batteries. And the light-emitting diode bulb will practically last forever.

Bring your own refillable water bottle. It's so easy to fall into the habit of buying bottled water when travelling—you don't want to get dehydrated during flights, you're not sure about the safety of the local water source. But bottled water is a massive eco-disaster, according to the Pacific Institute, requiring 17 million barrels of oil in manufacturing (not including transportation), producing more than 2.5 million tons of carbon dioxide, and using up three litres of water for each one-litre bottle. What's worse, the Union of Concerned Scientists says that 90 percent of water bottles are not recycled, so they will live out the next zillion years in a landfill.

Check out www.lifewithoutplastic.com to get yourself a lightweight aluminum or stainless steel travel bottle and tote your supply along with you. If local water potability is a concern, Mountain Equipment Co-op and other travel shops sell water purification tablets for travellers.

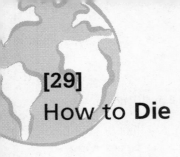

[29]
How to **Die**

It's not something we like to talk about, but the reality is it happens to all of us. And no matter how virtuous we may have been during our lifetime, being soaked with embalming fluid and lowered into the ground in a plastic-coated coffin will end things on a really bad note. But there are more natural ways to handle a body when it leaves this mortal coil. Here are a few things to remember when the time comes to deal with the death of a loved one.

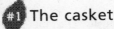 ## The casket

While you may want your dearly departed to have the best, remember that those plush satin interiors and polished veneer cases are really just for the benefit of those left behind. They certainly are not for the good of the earth. The chemicals used to treat and lacquer the wood, the synthetic foams and fabrics on the interior—those are full of petrochemicals, being put directly into the ground. And those metal handles and hinges will take forever to break down. The Ontario company Northern Caskets creates alternative caskets that keep conservation in mind. Check it out at www.northerncasket.com.

The body

According to the Natural Burial Association of Canada, the human body takes roughly 10 to 12 years to decompose. By putting a body into the ground in its natural state, that decomposition process can happen more readily. Even though that is hard to think about, it's really just the way nature is supposed to work. Embalming fluid is pretty much the opposite. Make specific arrangements with the funeral home to avoid the embalming process.

Natural burial grounds

The spooky cemetery, a mainstay of horror films and Scooby-Doo cartoons, is actually very real. Massive tombstones, created as monuments of significance by those left behind, begin to crumble and get lopsided over time, and ultimately fall into disrepair. Caskets are placed into concrete vaults to keep them from bumping into one another, and to keep the ground even to make it easier to mow the lawns. In addition to all that grass cutting, roads and walkways leading through the burial plots put an end to the natural life of the land so that eventually, when the plots are all full, there is no other possible use for the space—except to wind up as a scene in a scary movie.

In the early 1990s, a few groups in the UK decided to apply more holistic thinking to the notion of burials. As a result, natural burial grounds were created—areas of natural land staked out and protected for perpetuity. Natural burial grounds are not cluttered with marble headstones, involve no chemical embalming fluids going into the ground, and are filled with caskets and urns that are biodegradable. The body is returned to the earth in a truly natural way, marked with a specially planted tree or bush rather than a tombstone. To an unknowing passerby, a natural burial ground would look pretty much like a wild country meadow.

As a result, when all the plots are filled, the space is like a little green belt, ready to be handed over to a wildlife trust, so the natural beauty of a serene resting spot can be maintained for a long time.

There are more than 200 natural burial sites in the UK and 6 in the United States; several groups in Canada are planning to establish some here. For more information on planned Canadian sites, check out www.naturalburialassoc.ca.

#4 Cremation: not an eco-option

Many people assume that cremating a body is a less polluting way to dispose of it, but cremation is not without its environmental costs. British Columbia's chief medical officer says that cremation is a significant source of air pollution. Burning old dental fillings releases mercury into the air, and burning the rest of our bodies releases dioxin, hydrochloric acid, hydrofluoric acid, sulphur dioxide and carbon dioxide into the atmosphere. He recommends requiring environmental permits for crematoria and locating them away from urban centres to avoid the health risks to the public from inhaling particulate matter.

> BURIAL AT SEA To create a living memorial to someone who felt most at home on the ocean, a U.S. company will incorporate cremated remains into an artificial reef. Eternal Reefs is the only company that offers underwater burial at sea. By mixing cremated ashes with concrete, they create artificial reefs, which, over time, provide habitat for marine creatures and create a lasting environmentally friendly memorial (www.eternalreefs.com).

Making your wishes known

Have a conversation now with your family members, telling them you do not wish to be embalmed or have your casket put in a concrete vault. Request a casket made from locally sourced, sustainably harvested wood that is untreated—or cardboard for a less expensive option. Join the Memorial Society of British Columbia to learn more about facilitating a simple and affordable burial that promotes environmental conservation (www.memorialsociety.org). The first natural burial ground in Canada will open in fall 2008 as part of the Royal Oak Burial Park cemetery in Victoria. Several organizations are currently negotiating the land deals for other sites across Canada, including the Natural Burial Co-operative (www.naturalburial.coop/canada/).

[30]
How to **Do More**

If something in this book has inspired you to take action in your own life, I'm thrilled. I'll quietly celebrate your efforts, and I know you'll enjoy the good feeling that positive change always brings.

If taking action in your own life has inspired you to get more involved in the green movement, I'm ecstatic! I'll sing it from the treetops—and I'll see you at the Kyoto rallies.

#1 Make your homepage green

For useful, everyday green information that's interactive and updated, here are your best bets for websites:

www.treehugger.com: Started by a Canadian in 2003, TreeHugger has grown into what is perhaps North America's best-known environmental media outlet—it has been called the green CNN. Determined to make sustainable living the modern consumer reality, TreeHugger is a one-stop shop for all your green lifestyle questions and many more you haven't even thought of yet.

www.grist.org: If TreeHugger is the smart and enthusiastic enviro-class president, Grist is the snarky genius wisecracking at the back of the room. The picture of environmental news coverage and discussion would not be complete with either one missing. Grist is a non-profit organization serving up independent environmental journalism with a healthy dose of humour and cheek. Ask your tough eco-questions to Umbra, Grist's resident eco-guru. This one's my homepage.

www.environmentalhealthnews.org: As the devastating effects of pollution and global warming continue to mount, newspapers are reporting their fair share of stories relating to human health and the environment. But if you want your environmental health news served straight up without any distractions from Hollywood, the news-gathering service from Environmental Health Sciences is the place to turn. All health stories, all the time, from all around the world.

www.idealbite.com: The Ideal Bite is a daily e-service that delivers an enviro lifestyle tip by email. Their tips are useful for greening your everyday life, and witty and friendly in tone—it's kind of like getting a page of this book dropped into your inbox every day of the working week. Sign up for your free subscription at the website, where you can also search the full catalogue of all their tips since the company began in 2005.

BLACK IS THE NEW GREEN Make your search engine a little greener too. Blackle (www.blackle.com) is the official sister search engine of Google, but with black as the dominant colour onscreen. Since your computer's monitor requires more energy to light up a white screen than a black one, Blackle is a small step in the right direction. Making Blackle your regular search engine will serve as a daily reminder of the importance of being more earth-conscious, living up to the site slogan of "saving energy one search at a time."

Make your job green

If you've reached your threshold for pushing chlorine-bleached paper around a pressed wood desk in an overly air-conditioned office, set your green for life energies loose on a green gig. There are loads of great jobs to be had in the environmental sector, and while some may involve pushing paper, you can be darn sure it will be unbleached.

You wouldn't be the first to quit a meaningless job for a chance to help make the world a better place. Since 2001, GoodWork has been connecting and inspiring Canadians with opportunities for green employment. Check out www.goodworkcanada.ca.

 ## Make your free time count

You don't have to give up your day job to throw your considerable talents in the earth's direction. A little bit of your spare time can go a long way when it's harnessed by the right organization. To find out about which environmental organizations might benefit from your experience and energy, check out www.planetvolunteer.net. The earth has done so much for you, it'll feel great to give a little back.

 ## Get closer to the action

If you want to feel encouraged about where the planet is going, get acquainted with the many ENGOs that are its champions.

www.wwf.ca: World Wildlife Fund Canada is part of a global network of conservation organizations dedicated to improving living conditions for all the earth's species, including humans. The Canadian organization has conservation programs that focus on global warming, forests and freshwater, Pacific and Atlantic protected marine areas or eco-regions, Cuba, the Mackenzie Valley and species conservation.

www.greenpeace.ca: Greenpeace has long been the rebel among ENGOs, with its members risking their necks to draw attention to planetary crises around the world. Their tactics may not suit everyone's style, but these eco-warriors have enormously influenced the movement for environmental change around the world. Greenpeace Canada's work protects the boreal forest and the Great Bear Rainforest, as well as Canada's oceans. They have action campaigns to educate about climate change, genetic engineering, the Alberta tar sands and nuclear threats.

www.davidsuzuki.org: The David Suzuki Foundation allows the world's busiest environmental journalist to spread his message even further, through research and awareness-raising campaigns. The foundation is among the leading publishers of research on farmed fish (aquaculture), other impacts of the fishing industry, pesticide poisoning in Canada's North and sustainable economic development. Take the Suzuki Foundation's Nature Challenge and join a growing movement to make conservation part of your lifestyle.

www.sierraclub.ca: The Sierra Club of Canada is another supremely well-respected organization for environmental research and advocacy, the Canadian sister organization to the founding organization in the United States. The current leader of Canada's federal Green Party, Elizabeth May, earned her eco-stripes as head of the Sierra Club for more than a decade. Their programs include climate change, nuclear-free Canada, efforts to preserve precious water resources and species biodiversity, and education campaigns around our gluttonous energy consumption.

Get closer to the land

Lots of things make me wish I were 23 all over again—mostly the feeling I have when I try on new jeans. But nothing comes close to making me want to be childless and adventure-worthy again like the organization Willing Workers on Organic Farms (WWOOF). The Canadian chapter of this international organization connects well-intentioned non-farming types with opportunities to help out on a working organic farm. You can spend an extended period of time working there—kind of like a kibbutz, but without the carbon footprint of the flight to Israel. For those of us who are no longer 23 and footloose, there are farms who need volunteer help just for the day—you can go with the family to learn how organic farming works, help out milking the cows, even make maple syrup.

Check out www.wwoof.ca for listings of regional farms that are looking for volunteers. (Barbara Kingsolver's 2007 book *Animal, Vegetable, Miracle* is a mesmerizing chronicle of the author's experience moving her family to a farm in order to connect with the land and grow their own food. Great inspirational reading! If packing up your urban life to become a farmer isn't an option, WWOOF is the next best thing.)

 Vote with your vote

There's no doubt that individuals can a make massive impact by their collective choice. As anthropologist Margaret Mead famously said, "A small group of thoughtful people could change the world. Indeed, it's the only thing that ever has."

And while I would never have written this book if I didn't firmly believe that, I am also with David Suzuki when he says we have to bring our greenness with us when we step behind that propped-up cardboard shield on election day and cast our vote. An actively green citizenry can do a lot more when their government has the environment high on its agenda.

Nobel Prize–winning Canadian scientists have called our government's recent environmental policies "an international embarrassment" for their short-sightedness and lack of teeth.

Find out more about where your politicians stand on the environment; many organizations, like Greenpeace, the Sierra Club and the David Suzuki Foundation, rate and evaluate various party platforms, especially during election time.

#7 Tell all your friends

As any publicist will tell you, word of mouth is the single most valuable advertisement. You can be a powerful change agent within your community of friends, just by helping raise their eco-consciousness. You don't have to get preachy and moralistic—this is about *keeping* friendships after all. But talking up your latest green for life pursuits may spark someone else's interest—when they see how economical and rewarding your new-found green life is, they're sure to get on board too.

Acknowledgments

I always read the acknowledgments in books—I try to imagine the writer's life, friends and colleagues, and the story of how that particular book came into being.

These particular acknowledgments tell the story of this book, to be sure—from its inception at an organic juice bar, to its struggle for identity at the end of one helluva long television season, through a peaceful summer on the river and howling into a crammed season of writing and mothering in a whirlwind, around several tedious turns in the road meted out by downtown wallet thieves and hungry computers, up to its sunny conclusion, which you hold in your hands.

To all the characters in that story, I am grateful for your company in this little experiment in world betterment—you've certainly helped make *my* world a better place.

Foremost thanks to the woman who thought up the idea in the first place: thank you so much to Andrea Magyar for your patience and kindness guiding a broadcast gal through a paper medium, and for your particular empathy during all my peculiar missteps with the universe.

Immense thanks to the great and powerful Rosa Kim for such brilliant and thorough research—that baby will be green even before it gets here. Yippee. Thanks to Jennifer Dettman for having that great idea, among so many others.

253

Julie Bristow, you are a wise and brave woman—thank you for helping me see the value in doing this at a time when I couldn't see much very clearly. And thanks to Tim Falconer for such uncharacteristic common sense—you are a prince, and you certainly saved my summer.

Wonderful sources of green for life inspiration and knowledge made themselves available to me during this writing: thank you to Julie Daniluk for your organic wisdom, all-round support and the best eco-solution to a new wallet; to Brian Dockal for making beautiful, healthy, natural skin seem within reach; to Rob Grand for choosing to establish your wonderful eco-emporium right in my neighbourhood.

Muchas gracias to the venerable eco-connector Lee Schnaiberg, for being so terribly clever and for staying on top of that green ball no matter how fast it moves along.

A thousand bouquets of flowers for the lovely Ashlea Selskey for brokering the solutions to so many crises when you must have had enough of your boss's to deal with; awestruck appreciation to Brennan Last for reaching deep into the otherworld to pull out seven otherwise irretrievable chapters and get them back into my hands. And so many thanks to Andrea Hirsch and Sara Vinten for sharing your eyeballs at the eleventh hour.

Special thanks to the wonderful Deb Farquharson for your constant and gentle encouragement in so many of the pursuits written about here—for trying, with me, to be a green for life mum.

To two of my favourite writers, Esta Spalding and Craig Offman, for the votes of confidence—encouragement means a lot coming from such fabulous wordsmiths as you.

The longest ever hug of thanks to my delicious children who put up with a scatterbrained mum whose head was too full of natural cleaning recipes to keep track of her own wallet most of the time. Thank you for (mostly) staying out of my office, and also for readily embracing all the healthy toothpastes and natural foods we throw at you. We sure have tried to make you healthy—I hope you stay that way.

To my beloved Grant Gordon, endless thanks for so much encouragement and for regular kicks in the pants. Thank heavens for you, keeping your eye constantly on the moral imperative to do right by the earth and its people. If this book has half the reach and effect of the work you do, I will be thrilled.

Thanks to my mother, for teaching me to love and expect homemade food, and for the good sense to put on a sweater before turning up the heat. And thank you to my father, for teaching me to turn off the lights when I leave the room. I bet you never thought you'd hear me say that.

Invisible silent thanks to the Ottawa River for washing me and my family clean of our urban disconnect every summer. Hang on, big river. Hang on.

Index

Green for Life Notes

Green for Life Notes

Green for Life Notes

Green for Life Notes

Green for Life Notes

Green for Life Notes

Green for Life Notes